The Atlanta Exposition Cookbook

"Free Lunch," Cotton States and International Exposition, 1895. From a stereoscopic card in the collection of Michael Griffith, Atlanta, Georgia.

The Atlanta Exposition Cookbook

COMPILED BY
Mrs. Henry Lumpkin Wilson

INTRODUCTION BY
Darlene R. Roth

Brown Thrasher Books
THE UNIVERSITY OF GEORGIA PRESS
Athens

Paperback edition, 2012
Introduction by Darlene R. Roth © 1984
by the University of Georgia Press
Athens, Georgia 30602
www.ugapress.org
All rights reserved

Printed digitally in the United States of America

The Library of Congress has cataloged
the hardcover edition of this book as follows:
The Atlanta Exposition cookbook / compiled by Mrs. Henry
Lumpkin Wilson ; introduction by Darlene R. Roth.
xv, 148 p., [14] leaves of plates : ill. ; 20 cm.
Reprint. Originally published: Tested recipe cook book.
Atlanta : Foote & Davies Co., 1895.
"Brown thrasher books."
ISBN 0-8203-0708-4 (alk. paper)
1. Cooking—Georgia. 2. Atlanta (Ga.)—Social life
and customs. I. Wilson, Henry Lumpkin, Mrs. II. Title.
TX715.T35928 1984
641.59758—dc20   83-24252

Paperback ISBN-13: 978-0-8203-3945-0
ISBN-10: 0-8203-3945-8

The Atlanta Exposition Cookbook was first published in Atlanta,
Georgia, in 1895 under the title *Tested Recipe Cook Book*.

Contents

Introduction by Darlene R. Roth *vii*

Preface to the 1895 Edition *3*

Soups *5*

Oysters and Fish *9*

Meats *13*

Pickles *25*

Vegetables *29*

Salads *33*

Bread *39*

Cake *47*

Puddings and Custards *63*

Gelatines *78*

Chafing Dish Recipes *85*

Frozen Desserts *90*

Confectionery *100*

Beverages *104*

Menus *112*

P.S. *114*

Index *149*

Introduction

TO COOKS, a cookbook is many things—a guide to culinary expansion, an anthology of goodies, a mental taste-teaser, and a safety net in the school of experimentation. To cookbook lovers, a cookbook is all this and more—good reading, an invitation to other kitchens and imaginary feasts, and occasionally, as is the case with this cookbook, a historic event. I cook, I collect cookbooks, and I write history for a living, and I am delighted to introduce *The Atlanta Exposition Cookbook* as a tidy compendium of all these offerings. It should please all those who cook, who love to eat, who are intrigued with the origins of recipes and cooking methods, who love history—especially southern history— and who are openly curious about the stories southern women and their kitchens have to tell.

The Atlanta Exposition Cookbook was published at a time when cookbooks were relatively rare and often unreliable, though a variety of household manuals appeared with infrequent regularity in the United States after 1846, when Catharine Beecher (Harriet Beecher Stowe's sister) published *Miss Beecher's Domestic Receipt Book*. What is interesting about the Atlanta book is that it predates by a year the most famous American cookbook ever published, the *Boston Cooking-School Cook Book* by Fannie Merritt Farmer. Fannie Farmer modernized domestic cookery by printing exact measurements and cooking times in her book and by creating the now standard format for American recipe presentation: a list of measured ingredients followed by explicit cooking instructions. The value of the Farmer book lay in its obvious utility: with such streamlined procedures to follow, even the greenest cook could make dishes with some certainty of success.

The Atlantans who compiled this book were not as rigorous as Fannie Farmer, but they presaged her modernity. They presented their measured and tested recipes in an economy-conscious, efficient arrangement, organized into categories by type of dish. At the same time they adhered to an earlier style of recipe description (which persisted in Europe but not the United States) which relied on a disconcerting inexplicitness of direction. The recipes read in a kind of feminine shorthand that is both casual and intimate, as if the recipes were being spoken—knowingly, woman to woman. They regularly give exact measurements for ingredients but leave the cooking instructions vague, implied, or altogether absent. "Cook till done," "bake enough," and "bake quickly" are often all that is said.

The absence of times and temperatures, however, actually keeps this book current because 1895 cooking instructions would have been unsuitable for today's gas and electric ranges. As it is, modern cooks can easily translate the recipes, following rules for similar recipes from today's cuisine. The recipes given here are simple, some quite familiar, even when the names of dishes and ingredients seem old-fashioned (as well they should). The book, then, is still usable, with a little experience and common sense.

What the recipes lack in cooking instruction is more than compensated for by their personalization by the women who contributed them to the book, giving tips for their success. "If well made this mixture will keep good for weeks," says

Introduction

Mrs. Bussey of Atlanta about her imitation pâté de foie gras. Roast pigeons are "delightful for either dinner or supper" according to Mrs. Hobb of Albany, Georgia. Elsewhere a "splendid recipe" for chili sauce will "pay for [the] trouble" of making it. Serving instructions are numerous and entertaining to the modern reader, if not always useful. "Serve hot with plenty of rich cream" brings with it visions of some golden era when everyone was not on a diet, while "serve with wine sauce" reminds the reader that the South was not always restricted by prohibition, temperance, or even moderation.

The Atlanta Exposition Cookbook is historic for its modernity—given the early date of its appearance—and for its relative innovativeness among cookbooks of its era, but that only begins to tell its story.

This cookbook was issued at the 1895 Atlanta Cotton States and International Exposition by the Agricultural and Horticultural Committee of the Board of Women Managers. As a product of the Exposition, the book is illustrative of the women's efforts at the fair and a tribute to the agricultural base of southern economy at the time. The fair itself is a well-known moment in Atlanta history. Held between September 18 and December 31, 1895, it was described by its chronicler, Walter G. Cooper, as "Atlanta's greatest public enterprise," a description that probably still holds true. It stands out as one of Atlanta's most glamorous events and one of those self-conscious moments during which the city put forth its most assertive commercial foot. Officially, the fair was intended to stimulate trade and promote local recovery from the depression of the early 1890s; though the fair did not make as much money as its backers hoped, it did entertain more than eight hundred thousand visitors and offer some six thousand exhibits for their pleasure. The Exposition netted worldwide publicity for Atlanta and firmly established the city as the center of the Southeast in the minds of the country's financial and political leadership. The fair was a boon to the community in other ways as well, as the women's participation in it demonstrates.

The Board of Women Managers, composed of forty of the city's most prominent white women, oversaw all of the women's activities at the fair, except those that were held for black women in the Negro Building (for which there was a separate and very distinguished black women's committee). Women's activities included the exhibits by and about women in the Woman's Building, daily congresses and lectures on a wide spectrum of topics (from nutrition and painting to dress and professions), meetings of women's clubs from around the state and the nation, a demonstration kitchen, school, and kindergarten. The fair showcased the "progress" of southern women, celebrated their achievements as individuals, and attempted to reveal something of the nature of "Womanhood" in its totality—from the "lofty genius of Rosa Bonheur [a talented artist of the period] to the daintiest confection of real old southern housewifery." Some of those dainty confections appear in this cookbook, a collection of recipes taken from the kitchens of the Board of Women Managers and other women involved in the Exposition from around the state and other states. The Board sold the cookbook as a souvenir of the Exposition, drawing attention to the demonstrations in the model kitchen and raising

Introduction   ix

Introduction

funds to offset the costs of the Woman's Building, for which the Board supervised and financed the design, construction, furnishing, and maintenance.

This small volume is not just a cookbook, then, but a document in social history. It captures a point in history when southern kitchens were beginning to be rationalized and to admit new kinds of equipment, but they were still the province of domestic servants. While these recipes emanated from white kitchens, were tested and eaten in white homes, they were doubtless cooked by black servants. This helps to explain why the emphases here are on the quality of ingredients and the techniques for serving the food, not on the preparation itself. Just how acquainted the ladies of the Board were with food preparation is not known; probably every degree of familiarity is represented and may be inferred from the level of detail given in the recipes themselves. Some may have supervised in the kitchen; some may have ignored the process entirely; others may have cooked on special or private occasions. Some may have been heavily involved in the creation and recording of recipes; others not. It is known of one woman who contributed a recipe that she tried cooking only once and was so devastated by the experience—according to her daughter—that she never cooked again.

It is also not possible to know the full extent to which these women's kitchens were affected by increasingly available household technologies, but some clues are given. The compilers, for example, assume everyone is acquainted with the standard oven, but they take time to explain how best to use a chafing dish. In the 1890s, when this cookbook appeared, the improvements in kitchen management had more to do with questions of proper storage, efficient operation, and sanitation—all of which are referred to in passing throughout these pages—than appliances. The ice box is a common item to these women, but the refrigerator is still new. Presumably, all the stoves were wood-fired, as the gas stove as a standard kitchen feature took many decades to penetrate southern household economy, and it was well into the second and third decade of the twentieth century before gas ranges were at all common. In Atlanta this development is probably most closely identified with the career of Mrs. Henrietta Dull, for many years the food editor of the *Atlanta Constitution* and a consultant to the Atlanta Gas Company for the specific purpose of promoting gas ranges and instructing women how to use them. Her cookbook, *Southern Cooking*, published in 1941, is still a national classic.

It should be pointed out that the food described in these pages represents aspiring kitchen efforts and not simple southern fare. There are Sally Lunns and corn breads, but no grits; chicken dishes and ham, but no pork; pickled vegetables, but no greens; fancy gravies and sauces, but no pan juices. There are ices, ice creams, cakes, and gelatin desserts to suit the fanciest occasion, along with some uncommon international dishes. In a word, these recipes came from Atlanta's best kitchens, prescribed by its most society-conscious and prominent women.

In this lies the final point of historical significance in this book, for it constitutes a veritable roster of the Atlanta feminine elite and their friends. Here are the arbiters of society, the guardians of the social register, the models for decorum,

Introduction xiii

poise, and taste—wives of doctors, judges, bankers, businessmen, civic leaders, and politicians for whom hostessing social galas and intimate entertainments was a way of life.

Here also were the "New Women" of the 1890s who identified with social and political causes, formed women's organizations for social service and education, and became publicly visible in their community through their myriad clubs and societies. We take their efforts for granted today, but the women within these pages were the founders of the first women's organizations in Atlanta, the first activists, the first lobbyists. It is not possible to mention all of them or all of their many connections, but some of the names stand out: Mrs. E. L. Connally, wife of a West End doctor but also for thirty years a mainstay of the Baptist Orphans' Home; Mrs. William Lawson Peel, daughter of Confederate General Phillip Cook, and founder of both of Atlanta's DAR chapters (one in 1891 and the other in 1900); Mrs. Julius Brown, founder of the Atlanta Federation of Women's Clubs in 1899 and its first president; Mrs. Livingston Mime, who founded the First Christian Science Church in Atlanta in 1886 and selected its present site in 1913 just before her death; Mrs. W. A. Hemphill, who was bold enough to hold a reception for the National Woman's Suffrage Association in 1895 when Susan B. Anthony visited Atlanta, a time when woman suffrage was a daring and controversial idea in Atlanta; Mrs. James Jackson, an officer and leader for many years in the Georgia Federation of Women's Clubs, the Atlanta Woman's Club, and the YWCA; Mrs. W. G. Raoul, a lobbyist and supporter for the Atlanta Free Kindergarten Association, an interest of hers that spanned decades of activity; Mrs. Rebecca

Lowe, founder of the Atlanta Woman's Club (1895), the Georgia Federation of Women's Clubs (1896), and national president of the General Federation of Women's Clubs (1898–1902); Mrs. Archibald Davis, the first president of woman's work for the Presbyterian Church of the U.S., a local and national official of the YWCA, and one of the founders of the women's division of the Commission on Inter-racial Cooperation in 1920; and last, but certainly not least, the variously famous and notorious gadfly of southern politics, Rebecca Latimer Felton (Mrs. William H.), who was a lecturer, teacher, writer, suffragette, and political activist for many controversial causes, and who became the first woman ever to sit in the United States Senate.

The Atlanta Exposition of 1895 provided these women with a showground for their growth and a forum for their activities; it also served to accelerate the club movement in Atlanta, offering a meeting ground of the first order for everyone from presswomen to nurses to patriots and hospital volunteers. Several organizations, such as the Atlanta Section of the National Council of Jewish Women, were actually founded at the Exposition; others met in statewide conference for the first time. The Atlanta Woman's Club (white) and a black counterpart were formed as a direct outgrowth of the women's involvements at the Exposition.

The Atlanta Exposition Cookbook, therefore, which could quite easily be dismissed as a collection of old recipes for things people do not eat anymore (like terrapins and pigeons) and of highly caloric dishes that people do not think they *should* eat anymore, is actually a document of very special importance, signifying the origins of a long southern tra-

Introduction xv

dition tying women, women's public activities, and food together. I like to see this book as a sister to Fannie Farmer, a mother to Mrs. Dull, and a grandmother to a ubiquitous contemporary phenomenon, the clubwomen's cookbook, made popular by the success of *Charleston Receipts*, published by the Charleston Junior League in 1950, and replicated hundreds of times since across the country.

Read, eat, and enjoy.

DARLENE R. ROTH
Atlanta, Georgia

MRS. HENRY LUMPKIN WILSON,
Chairman Committee on Agriculture and Horticulture.

TESTED RECIPE
COOK BOOK.

COMPILED BY

MRS. HENRY LUMPKIN WILSON,

Chairman Committee on Agriculture and Horticulture, Board of Women Managers Cotton States and International Exposition.

ATLANTA, GA.

"The body craveth meats and the spirit is athirst for peacefulness. He that hath these hath enough."—*Tupper.*

ATLANTA:
THE FOOTE & DAVIES COMPANY.
1895.

COPYRIGHT, 1895,
BY MRS. HENRY LUMPKIN WILSON.

PREFACE.

No recipe is of value until it has been tested. Conversely, every recipe wisely endorsed is of much value. In offering to the public, therefore, these various concoctions, endorsed by names well-known throughout Georgia and the South, Mrs. Henry L. Wilson, the compiler of this little volume, and herself a recognized authority on household matters, has wrought a good work.

Moreover, this enterprise, undertaken by the Chairman of the Committee on Agriculture and Horticulture, in behalf of that department, is happily appropriate. For it is the field and the garden which feed the larder and the table; and Ceres and Pomona, for all their classic names and lineage, are but the constant ministers to that homely Saxon syllable which we know as cook.

Believing, therefore, that this book will go forth to win a wide success, is only believing that the eternal fitness of things will be accomplished. For it is but meet that these golden recipes, coined by skilled housewives from the distant mint of farm and field, should be the emissaries to go out and gather in a return treasury of gold for their original benefactors—Agriculture and Horticulture.

Ernel Jay

RECIPE FOR MAKING A HOME HAPPY.

One ounce each system, frugality and industry, one ounce each gentleness, patience and forbearance, six ounces Paul's Christian charity, that covers a multitude of failures. These ingredients thoroughly kneaded with the salt of good common sense, flavored with the "graces of nature and art," music and flowers, will make a paradise of a desert, a palace of a hovel.—Mrs. S. C. Ferrell, LaGrange, Ga. (Ferrell's Gardens.)

RECIPE FOR CHEERFULNESS.

(The best flavor known to mortals.) Take two parts of unselfishness, add as much fresh air as can easily be obtained, stir in two hours of "beauty sleep," a silver tongue (from the tip of which all spite has been removed), and an eye that looks out on the brighter side of life. Into this mixture throw a pinch of humor and a sprinkle of the essence of romance. The result is cheerfulness warranted to stand the test of time. Where is the mental and moral kitchen which furnishes to life's table this wholesome food?—Miss Mary L. Jackson, Atlanta.

RECIPES.

SOUPS.

BEEF is the best meat to be used, and only cold water should be used at first; then if more water be used let it be hot. One of the best articles for young or old housekeepers to keep on hand is a can of good extract of beef. With a little hot water, a bowl of very rich soup can be made at a moment's notice. It requires but a spoonful of the extract for a bowl of soup; can be made in five minutes. In point of time, strength and money, it cannot be excelled. Give variety by change of flavoring, as celery, wine, catsup, and onions, etc.

Bouillon.—Ten pounds of round steak, cut up in small pieces, take off all the fat; put the meat in a vessel and cover with water; let it boil ten hours, keeping meat covered with water; add one lemon, cut up, and two tablespoons bay leaves; pepper and salt to taste; strain through a thick cloth, put on the stove again. When it begins to boil add the whites of two eggs well beaten. Strain and serve. This amount will be sufficient for twelve persons.—Mrs. W. D. Grant, Atlanta.

Celery Soup.—One pint of milk, one tablespoon of flour, one head of celery, one small onion and a half teaspoon of mace. Boil celery in a pint of water thirty minutes. Boil onions, milk and mace together. Mix flour with two tablespoons of milk. Cook all together ten minutes. Add the butter, and season with salt and pepper. Stirring, add a cupful of whipped cream. Serve immediately.—Mrs. Burton Smith, Atlanta.

Creole Gumbo.—One chicken, cut up, one quart okra, six large onions, twelve large tomatoes. Have okra and onions sliced fine. Fry the chicken first, and then in the same skillet fry the okra and onions. Put all in a soup pot and add two quarts of boiling water, and the tomatoes, the two slices of boiled ham cut up fine, red and black pepper. Serve with rice, boiled dry. Oysters are a great addition to the gumbo. —Mrs. C. C. Black, "Deerland."

Ground-pea Soup.—Shell one quart of roasted ground-peas, rub off the dry, brown skin carefully, pound the nuts to a smooth paste in a mortar, gradually stir into it one quart of fresh sweet milk, let it simmer gently until it thickens, stirring frequently to prevent burning. Add to this one quart of oysters, drained, a little cayenne pepper and salt to taste. As soon as the oysters are sufficiently cooked, serve.—Mrs. Frank H. Orme, Atlanta.

Gumbo Fillet.—This can be made of either chicken, oysters or crabs. Fry your chicken, also a dozen onions, put in the soup pot, pour over them two quarts of boiling water, add some boiled ham, cut up fine. Fifteen minutes before you take it up, add your oysters. When they are plump, put in two tablespoons of fillet, dissolved in cold water. Serve with rice.

Fillet.—Take young sassafras leaves, dry them in the shade; when crisp break them up and sift them through a fine sieve, or piece of muslin.—Mrs. Neville Black, New Orleans.

Mock Turtle.—Put one beef bone to simmer (not to boil) in a small stone vessel of water for two hours. Have ready some flour, browned. Add one teacup of browned flour mixed to a smooth paste, six cloves, one teaspoon of celery seed, red and black pepper to taste. Put no salt in the soup until it is nearly ready to send to the table. If liked, add tomato catsup and wine. Always skim off grease as it rises. —Mrs. M. G. Holliday, Aberdeen, Miss

Chicken Gumbo.—Put in a soup pot one tablespoon of sifted flour, and the same of lard. Let it become a rich brown; add one chicken, cut up; season with salt, pepper, onions and a little tomato. Pour into this two quarts of hot water. Let boil two hours. Thirty minutes before serving, add one quart of oysters, one tablespoon of mashed bay leaves, and one tablespoon of butter. Serve hot.—Mrs. D. N. Speer, Atlanta.

Mock Bisque Soup.—One quart of milk, a large tablespoon of butter, one bay leaf, one-fourth teaspoon of soda, a blade of mace, one pint cream tomatoes, a sprig of parsley, one teaspoon sugar, three tablespoons of flour. Put the tomatoes in a saucepan with the bay leaf, parsley and mace, cover and stand on back of stove fifteen minutes. Put the milk in a double boiler, put the butter and flour together, add the milk and stir until it thickens. Strain the tomatoes and put into the soup tureen. Add sugar and soda, pour in quickly the boiling milk, stir and serve immediately. If not ready to serve, keep both tomatoes and milk hot, separately, then mix and add the soda and sugar just the moment needed.—Mrs. Loulie M. Gordon, Atlanta.

Oyster Soup.—Two quarts oysters, two quarts milk, one tablespoon butter, two of sifted flour, one and one-half wineglass of sherry wine, a few blades of mace and pepper. Boil the milk and stir in the flour and butter already creamed together, then add the oysters; when done add the wine, drop by drop, to prevent curdling. Dish and serve immediately. —Mrs. Wm. H. Atwood, McIntosh Co., Ga.

Lenten Soup.—Wash one-fourth pound small sago in cold water, put it on the fire in three quarts cold water, with a level teaspoon of salt, as much cayenne pepper as can be held on the point of a small knife blade, a saltspoon of grated nutmeg. Stir the sago frequently to prevent burning. Cook until entirely transparent, adding more water, if required. When the sago is transparent add one-fourth pound sugar and boiling water to make three quarts of soup, then put in a quart of claret, or any good domestic red wine, and stir it until dissolved. When soup is cold serve it, or ice it and serve cold.—Mrs. James Wotton, "West End."

Cream Tomato Soup.—One can of tomatoes, one pint milk, one pint hot water, one-half teaspoon salt, one teaspoon soda, one-fourth spoon pepper. Melt in another vessel one tablespoon of butter and when hot, add one tablespoon of flour. Cook a few minutes, then add one cup of milk, slowly stirring all the time. Cook till smooth and creamy. Rub tomatoes through strainer, adding hot water slowly, then soda; put both together and add rest of milk. Let all reach boiling point. Serve hot.—Mrs. S. P. Callaway, LaGrange, Ga.

Cream or Corn Soup.—One can grated corn, one and one-half pints hot water, one tablespoon butter, one flour, one pint hot milk, one teaspoon salt, one-fourth pepper. Melt the butter and when hot and bubbling add the flour, cook until frothy, stirring constantly. Add slowly the milk, stir and add the corn, with hot water, salt and pepper. Serve immediately.—Mrs. Harriet E. Johnson, Inman Park.

OYSTERS AND FISH.

Fish Pudding.—Take any kind of fish you like. Salmon or trout is best. Put on and boil fifteen minutes. Take off and pick up fine. Make a cream sauce as for chicken croquettes. Put a layer of fish and one of sauce, until your baking dish is full. Put on top a layer of grated cheese and bread crumbs. Bake until brown and serve with cream sauce.

Cream Sauce.—One pint cream, two pounds butter, two tablespoons of flour. Put butter in a saucepan and melt. Put in your flour. Stir in your flour until well mixed, then pour over your cream and stir until it thickens.—Mrs. Hoke Smith, Washington, D. C.

Oyster Coquille.—Chop oysters rather fine. To one quart add two hard-boiled eggs, two raw eggs, well beaten, a small quantity of minced pickle, one tablespoon lemon juice, three-fourths teacup butter. Pepper and salt to taste. Thicken with crumbs of toasted bread. Put on stove and let it get thoroughly heated, stirring constantly. Bake in shells, with crumbs on top.—Mrs. S. B. Hudson, Columbus, Miss.

Creamed Oysters.—To one quart of cream use one quart oysters; let the cream come to a boil; thicken with cracker dust, until of the consistency of pudding batter; season with pepper and salt. Pour in the oysters and keep on stove until hot through. Then place in oven and bake. If cream is not obtainable, milk can be used with addition of fresh butter.—Mrs. Alex. Smith, Atlanta.

Pickled Oysters.—To every quart of large, fresh oysters add one pint apple vinegar, one tablespoon cloves, one of allspice, one teaspoon of salt. Add no water to oysters. Wash them and let come to a boil, pour over vinegar and spices. Add salt and let all come to a boil, and when cold

Oysters and Fish.

they are ready to serve. Use no ground spices.—Mrs. Stokes Gregory, Atlanta.

Mock Oysters.—One can of corn chopped fine, two well beaten eggs, one cup milk, butter—size of an egg—salt and pepper. Thicken with a little flour and fry in hot lard.—Miss Nettie Sergeant, Atlanta.

Fish a la Creme.—Take any kind of fish—boiled. Pick the fish to pieces, taking out the bones; place in a baking dish. Beat together a tablespoon of butter and a little flour. Pour on this a pint of boiling cream, stir smooth and season with salt and pepper, yolks of two eggs, well beaten. Pour over the fish, grate a little cheese over the top and bake twenty minutes.—Mrs. E. T. Cook, Montgomery, Ala.

Deviled Crabs.—For one dozen persons use one large can of crabs, taking care to first remove all those hard particles which may be in it. Take three eggs, beaten separately, mix them, then stir in the crabs, one tablespoon at a time, until all of the crabs are used. Then add the juice of a half lemon, three tablespoons melted butter, one teaspoon salt and one-third spoon red pepper, two tablespoons cracker crumbs. Put in the shells and cover with cracker crumbs mixed with a little butter. Bake in hot oven a few minutes.—Mrs. Grant Wilkins, Atlanta.

Hardshell Crabs.—Remove meat from four dozen hard-shelled crabs and chop up fine. Put in a saucepan one onion, cut up in small pieces, and one ounce butter. When beginning to color slightly add a dozen chopped mushrooms, a tablespoon of chopped parsley and four ounces hard crumbs, previously soaked in consomme, and then pressed almost dry, a small pinch of salt and pepper, a little cayenne, and half a gill of tomato sauce. Mix all well together and cook for five minutes. Wash the shells and fill them with the mixture, cover with hard crumbs and a very little melted butter on top. Send to the oven and color a light brown.—Mrs. Lyden-Meekin, Baltimore, Md.

Shrimps in Bell Peppers.—A soup plate of freshly-picked shrimps, cut a little (not chop), dust them with a little nutmeg and black pepper, then add to them a teacup of rich cream and a tablespoon piled with butter, then add a teacup, scant, of grated bread crumbs (not toasted crumbs), and lastly a wineglass of sherry wine. Place in peppers that have been in cold water for two hours, sprinkle lightly with crumbs, place in a pan and bake.—Miss Mary A. Garrard, Isle of Hope.

Deviled Shrimp.—One can shrimp, one can tomatoes, one tablespoon butter; red or black pepper and salt to taste. Stew tomatoes and when nearly done, season. Mince shrimp and add to tomatoes, mixing thoroughly. A half cup of tomato catsup is an improvement. Cover the whole with cracker dust and brown on top.—Mrs. James LeConte Anderson, Macon, Ga.

Baked Salmon.—Put in water to soak about two slices of stale bread, then press water out thoroughly; into the bread put one-fourth teaspoon red pepper, one-half teaspoon salt, two tablespoons of Worcestershire sauce, one tablespoon of melted butter, parsley, or celery tops, to taste. Mix all thoroughly; break into the mixture three (or more) eggs and beat up lightly. Put into this one can salmon steak and stir enough to mix thoroughly with bread, etc.; use a light touch in mixing. Place in a well-buttered pan, put a few pieces of butter over top and bake until brown.—Mrs. Julius Alexander, Atlanta.

Turbot a la Creme.—Boil your fish with plenty of salt, remove bones and flake it in as large pieces as you can. Boil one quart cream, stirring into it three tablespoons fish until smooth, one large onion, a small bunch parsley, let boil five minutes, then take parsley and onion out and add a quarter pound melted butter. Butter a deep dish; put in a layer of fish, then one of cream, then a thin layer of cheese, alternating until dish is full. Cream comes on top. Then a layer of bread crumbs and cheese. Garnish dish with parsley. Any fish free from bones can be used.—Mrs. Charles Hopkins, Atlanta.

Fillet of Flounder a la Joinville.—Skin two flounders and cut the flesh from the bones with a sharp knife. There will be eight fillets, which must be rolled into eight little turbans and each fastened with a wooden toothpick. Put into the dish one ounce of butter and when it bubbles add fish. Cover closely and let them simmer a few minutes; then add a small glass of cider champagne, one small onion, a little lemon juice, three pepper corns and a pinch of salt, and simmer again till done. Remove the fish, thicken the juice with one ounce of butter well rubbed with one tablespoon flour, and strain it over the fillets. A very nice addition is to have some oysters cooked in their own juice with which to trim the fillets.—Mrs. Robert Collins, Atlanta.

Steamed Salmon.—One lean salmon, four eggs beaten light, four tablespoons butter melted but not hot, one-half cup fine bread crumbs, seasoned with pepper, salt and parsley. Chop fish fine and rub butter into it until smooth; beat the crumbs

MRS. JOSEPH THOMPSON,
President Board of Women Managers Cotton States and International Exposition.

into the eggs and season before working together. Put into a buttered mold and steam one hour.

Sauce.—One cup sweet milk heated to a boil, thickened with one tablespoon corn starch and one tablespoon butter rubbed together, the liquor from salmon, one raw egg, one tablespoon of tomato catsup, a pinch of cayenne pepper and mace; add milk carefully.—Miss Marion H. May, Atlanta.

Diamond Back Terrapin.—Select females seven inches under bottom of shell; place alive in boiling water. When upper and lower shell easily separate, carefully remove the gall from the large lobe of the liver, by making a deep incision entirely around the gall sac to prevent its bursting. Next remove the lungs, which are under the upper portion of the back, on the top shell. Everything else is eatable. Place in a chopping dish, add cayenne pepper, salt and butter to taste. Bring to a boiling point, add heated champagne, sherry, or old Madeira. Serve hot.—Mrs. Frederick F. Lyden, Baltimore.

MEATS.

TO SERVE WITH MEAT AND FISH.

Roast beef should be served with grated horse-radish.
Roast mutton with currant jelly.
Boiled mutton with caper sauce.
Roast pork with apple sauce.
Roast lamb with mint sauce and green peas.
Venison or wild duck with black currant jelly.
Roast goose with apple sauce, or cranberries.
Roast turkey with oyster sauce and cranberries.
Roast chicken with bread sauce and apple jelly.

Compote of pigeon with mushroom sauce.
Broiled fresh mackerel with sauce of stewed cranberries.
Broiled bluefish with white cream sauce.
Broiled shad with rice.
Fresh salmon with green peas and cream sauce.

Chicken Coquille.—Boil a chicken as for salad. When taken out of the pot, save a little of the stock. Cut the meat into small squares, put into a dish and cover with sherry. Put a cupful of milk to boil, then take one tablespoon of flour, one tablespoon of butter, add this to the milk. While boiling, stir constantly. Into this put mushrooms, one cupful, a little of the stock, put chicken, mushrooms and milk into a dish and mix thoroughly. After putting into shells sift bread crumbs on each, then put in oven and brown slightly.—Mrs. R. T. Bishop, Montgomery, Ala.

Creole Stew.—Put into the stewpan one-half onion cut fine, one teaspoon of flour, one can of tomatoes, pepper and salt to taste, one and one-half cups water. Into this put one chicken, cut up as for frying. Sift flour lightly over the chicken, and let the whole remain for one hour (do not let it boil). Then it is ready for use, to be served with rice, which has been boiled until each grain stands alone. Serve the rice first on the plate and put the stew over it. Dinner dish.—Mrs. W. A. Hemphill, Atlanta.

Stuffed Mutton Chops.—Select loin chops, cut one and one-half inches thick, and trim them closely. With a sharp-pointed knife make a pocket in each, reaching to the backbone. Fill with a forcemeat of sausage and bread crumbs, adding more seasoning to taste. Fasten the mouth of the pocket with a toothpick skewer. Broil them on each side until well browned, then set into a hot oven for six minutes. To be served with the following sauce: Mix one tablespoon vinegar, one teaspoon lemon juice, one saltspoon salt, one tablespoon Worcestershire sauce, and heat over hot water. Brown one-third cup butter. Strain it into the mixture and pour at once over the chops.—Mrs. J. D. Collins, Atlanta.

Tongue Croquettes.—Mix one cup of cold tongue, chopped fine; one cup of cold mashed potatoes. Put this mixture in a saucepan. Stir over the fire until the potatoes are soft. Add one unbeaten egg. Mix carefully, dip in the yellow of one egg, roll in cracker dust, make in shapes and fry in boiling lard.—Mrs. B. G. Swanson, LaGrange, Ga.

Birds Dressed with Mushrooms.—Prepare the birds as if they were to be broiled. Put them in a chafing dish, or roaster with top. To a dozen birds put a cup of water. A lump of butter on each bird. A little red pepper. When half done add salt, a little flour to thicken the gravy, half a pint of port wine, tablespoon of Worcestershire sauce and the juice of one lemon. It requires about three or four hours to cook.—Mrs. Rhode W. Hill, Atlanta.

Champagne Sauce for Ham.—One tablespoon of sugar, one wineglass of vinegar. Put in saucepan on fire to boil until reduced one-half. Add one quart of chicken broth, one glass sherry. Boil about five or ten minutes and it is ready to use over sliced cold boiled ham.—Miss Anna Lumpkin, Lebanon, Tenn.

Meats.

Grillard.—In two tablespoons of hot lard put two rounds of veal steak, cut thin, with one teaspoon flour sifted over it. When brown add one small onion, cut fine; one-half dozen or one-half can tomatoes. Stir often, add red pepper and salt to taste. Cover closely. In twenty minutes, when brown, add one-half pint of water. Cook slowly one hour. Serve with rice.—Mrs. Florine Holt, Atlanta.

Recipe for Quails.—Dress sixteen quails as you would a chicken to bake. Put in roasting pan with a little hot water. Piece of butter on each bird. Teacup of port wine, two tablespoons of Worcestershire sauce, red pepper pod. Cut in strips over the birds and salt to taste. Cook two hours in closely-covered pan. Boil two-pound can small mushrooms until tender. Do not let water on birds become exhausted. After they have cooked one hour add mushrooms. Just before serving, thicken with flour and milk. Serve all on one dish with parsley.—Mrs. James English, Atlanta.

Cranberries.—One quart cranberries, one scant quart granulated sugar, one pint cold water. Wash the berries well, put in granite saucepan, pour the water over them and set on back of stove where they will cook slowly. When they are softly boiling add one-fourth of the sugar, pressing the berries down, but not stirring them. When the sugar has melted add another one-fourth and so on until the sugar is all used and turned to syrup. Do not on any account stir the fruit. When the berries are soft and clear they are done.—Miss Josephine Inman, Atlanta.

Maitre d'Hotel Butter.—A delightful sauce to pour over a broiled bird, chicken or fish. Mix together cold, one ounce

Meats.

of butter, a tablespoon of chopped parsley, a teaspoon of lemon juice and one-fourth saltspoon of salt.—Mrs. Lila P. Hull, Atlanta.

Syrian Dish (Yabrah).—One pound mutton in small bits, one-half pound rice washed seven times. Mix and season to taste with pepper and salt. Take large head of cabbage, pick the leaves separately, scald thoroughly and cut away the heavy parts. Make the leaves in pieces four or five inches square, and into each piece put about a dessert spoon of the meat and roll tightly like a cigarette. Pack tightly in saucepan and cover with hot water. Let boil hard one hour. Just before removing from the fire pour in the juice of three lemons. When grape leaves can be had, use in preference to cabbage.—Miss Sophie David, Damascus, Syria.

Lamb's Head Stew.—Take the head, skin it or scrape it, either one; then split it open and put it to boil with the liver, the lights and the heart. Let all boil until tender; then cut it up fine. If there are any bones in the pot take them out, and before you add the meat to the liquid again thicken it with a little browned flour and color it with a little burnt sugar, seasoning it with mace, cloves and allspice. Return your cut-up meat to the liquid, boil up and serve with wine and quartered lemons.—Miss Sallie L. Wylly, Darien, Ga.

Stewed Kidneys with Mushrooms.—Boil your kidneys or a small calf's liver five or six hours. Let it stand until the following day, cut it into small dice and put to cook in a quart of water. Boil an hour, and just before serving season high with salt, black and red pepper. Then add a pint of canned mushrooms, a tablespoon of butter, a tablespoon of lemon juice, two tablespoons of rum or sherry wine and a small piece of lemon peel. Thicken with a tablespoon of corn starch mixed in a little water, and serve.—Mrs. Harry Jackson, Atlanta.

Boiled Ham.—Soak the ham in water one night; then boil in water and one pint of white wine vinegar. Allow it to get cold in its own liquor; then skin, sprinkle sugar over top and bake until brown.—Mrs. Warren Akin, Cartersville, Ga.

Thanksgiving Turkey.—For one plump, young turkey allow one-half pound of bread crumbs, one-half pound of suet, a small bunch of parsley, three small onions, one and one-half pints of cream, two tablespoons of flour, seasoning, one teacup of milk, six whole tomatoes and the juice of six, one-half pound butter. After washing turkey thoroughly inside and out, and allowing it to become quite dry, dust lightly with flour. Suet, carefully shredded, must be chopped fine with parsley and onion. Add this to the bread crumbs and season with salt, pepper and a dash of nutmeg. This mixture must be moistened with one pint of cream and mixed up into balls an inch or more in circumference. Use tomatoes that have been put up whole and proceed to fill the turkey with tomatoes, alternating with one ball, until quite full. Into a saucepan put the juice of the other six tomatoes, one-half pound of butter, seasoning and a teaspoon of flour, and allow to simmer slowly until it thickens. When the turkey is first basted, throw the whole of the sauce well over it, continuing to baste the fowl until brown and crisp. The gravy is made by pouring balance of cream and milk into the dripping, which put back into the oven and keep until it boils well. Place in a gravy bowl. Serve both sauce and turkey very hot.—Mrs. M. C. Kiser, Atlanta.

Brain Patties.—For twelve patties put two sets of brains and one box of mushrooms. Boil brains done. Take off and put in clear water and lemon juice. Chop up mushroom and brains together, add tablespoon of butter, half a cup of cream, stew a few moments with pepper, salt and nutmeg to taste. Serve hot in patties.—Mrs. E. P. Black, Atlanta.

Imitation Pate de Foie Gras.—Boil one pound of calf liver in slightly salted water until quite tender. Pound the liver in mortar, moistening from time to time with melted butter, seasoning well with cayenne pepper, made mustard, grated nutmeg and add a tablespoon of water in which has been boiled one onion and one clove. When well mixed pack in small jelly pots and pour melted butter over the surface. Small triangular bits of liver and gizzards of fowls, and bits of tongue may be inserted here and there to imitate the truffle found in the genuine Strasburg patties. If well made this mixture will keep good for weeks.—Mrs. Sauloel McKinley Bussey, Atlanta.

Beef a la Daube.—Four pounds of beef, the round. Pierce it with a knife and in the place slip slices of bacon. Flour it and brown it well; then cover it with boiling water, adding twelve onions chopped fine, dessert spoon of allspice, parsley, thyme and bay leaves. Boil for four hours. Thicken the gravy with brown flour.—Mrs. Alex. King, Atlanta.

Apple Duck.—Take one dozen firm, glossy, acid apples. With a penknife make a round hole in the bloom end of each, size of a silver quarter. With an orange spoon carefully remove the cores and insides, having an even thickness of an inch next to the skin. Have one pint of cold duck (chicken or veal may be used) chopped fine with boiled brains of a calf. For every pint of this meat allow a half pint of rich milk, tablespoon of butter, two tablespoons of flour, tablespoon of chopped parsley, a little grated nutmeg, a dash of cayenne. Put the milk on to boil. Thicken it with the butter and flour, rub together, take from the fire, mix and cream, adding the meat. Fill the apple shell with this mixture. Sprinkle bread on top of opening, small piece on each. Bake until well done, but not too soft. Garnish with parsley. Serve with bread sticks as a course, luncheon, or tea.—Mrs. A. J. Orme, Atlanta.

Roast Pigeons.—Select large fat birds just ready to fly. Dress birds for stuffing. For twelve birds take one-half a loaf of light bread, moisten with sweet milk, add a quarter of a pound of butter, red and black pepper and salt to taste. Cut fine a small box of truffles and add to dressing. Stuff the birds with this and put them to roast, keeping them constantly basted with a sauce made of one-half cup Worcestershire and nearly one-half pound butter. Cook for about an hour or longer. These are delightful for either dinner or supper.—Mrs. Annie Tarver Hobbs, Albany, Ga.

Sauce for Roast Lamb and Mutton.—Two tablespoons Worcestershire sauce, two of wine, four of vinegar, small pieces of butter, mustard, pepper and salt to taste; add a small quantity of lamb gravy, warm until the butter melts. —Miss Delphine Force, St. Louis, Mo.

MRS. LOULIE M. GORDON,
Representative at Large and Chairman Committee on Woman's Congresses.

Chicken Terrapin.—Cream together one tablespoon of butter and flour. Put in a saucepan with a large cupful of cream or milk. When it comes to a boil, stir in one-half can of mushrooms cut in quarters; then a soup plate of minced turkey or chicken. Season with nutmeg, cayenne pepper, salt, and lastly, a large claret glass of sherry. Serve either in pastry shells or brown twenty minutes in a baking dish.—Mrs. Billups Phinizy, Augusta, Ga.

Chicken Croquettes.—One pint of very finely-chopped chicken, four eggs boiled hard, with a little onion and a little parsley mixed with the chicken, pinch of salt and pepper, two tablespoons of tomato sauce, butter size of an egg, one-half cup of sweet milk or a beaten raw egg. Mold them in a wine glass; then roll them in beaten egg, and then in cracker dust. Fry in a deep vessel in very hot lard.—Mrs. William Rawson, Atlanta.

Stuffed Ham.—Boil your ham until done, remove the skin and with a sharp knife make incisions in it to the bone, lengthways of the ham. Then make dressing of light bread soaked in milk, one onion, a little butter, celery seed, red and black pepper. Mix thoroughly and stuff the incisions you have made in ham. Grate cracker crumbs over the ham, return to the oven and let brown.—Mrs. Marion Lumpkin Wilson.

Marrow Fritters.—(Served with Beefsteak.) Get from the butcher several pieces of marrow in as large pieces as possible. Boil them in a shallow pan, a little salt, for a minute. Drain away the water very carefully, add a good pinch of pepper and a teaspoon of chopped parsley. Let the batter be stiff and drop by spoonfuls into boiling lard. When light brown lift out and make a border of them around broiled steak.—Miss June McKinley, Atlanta.

Delicious Stuffing for Fowls.—Two dozen oysters. Chop them fine and mix with bread crumbs one full ounce of butter, one tablespoon of chopped parsley, a little grated lemon peel, one teaspoon of salt, one of black pepper, a little cayenne pepper. The great secret of cooking is to have the ingredients so blended that it is impossible to tell of what it is composed. Moisten the stuffing a little with hot milk beaten with yolk of one egg.—Mrs. Annie Shoecraft, Rochester, N. Y.

Patties au Salpicon.—One pint cupful of chicken cut in dice, one pint cupful of rich cream sauce, pinch of parsley chopped fine. The chicken having been prepared as for salad, put into a saucepan, season with white pepper or cayenne, a grating of nutmeg, the juice of one-half lemon, little salt, and one ounce of butter. Next pour over it the cream sauce and let it gently simmer at the back of a range until time to dish up; then fill the pattie cases with mixture. —Mrs. P. H. Snook, Atlanta.

For Boiling Ham.—Take a ham weighing from fifteen to eighteen pounds, wash thoroughly, and put it to boil with water sufficient to cover it, into which a pint of vinegar has been poured. Boil three hours. When half the time has expired, turn over. Remove the skin, trim nicely, place in a dripping pan, and pour a pint of vinegar over it. Take the yolk of an egg and beat into it a cupful of brown sugar. With a knife spread this over the ham until all the top is covered. Bake one-half an hour, then baste with the vinegar. This gives a flavor like champagne.—Mrs. George T. Fry, Sr., Chattanooga, Tenn.

Creamed Chicken.—One chicken of four and one-half pounds, or two of three pounds, and four pounds sweetbreads, a can of mushrooms. Boil chicken and sweetbreads, and when cool, cut up as if for salad. In a saucepan put a quart of cream or new milk; in another, four large table spoons of butter and five even ones of flour. Stir till melted, and then pour over hot cream. Stir until it thickens. Flavor with one-half small onion grated, and a very little nutmeg grated. Season highly with black and red pepper. Put chicken in saucepan, all in baking dish, cover with bread crumbs and several pieces of butter. Bake ten or twenty minutes until done. For twelve persons.—Mrs. A. G. Blincoe, Bardstown, Ky.

Veal a la Mode.—Three and one-half pounds of round of veal chopped fine, three eggs, one-half cup milk, butter size of an egg, four crackers rolled fine, two teaspoons salt, one teaspoon pepper, one grated nutmeg. Mix thoroughly, make into loaf and bake one hour.—Mrs. James F. Leary, Atlanta.

Sweetbreads.—Parboil and place them in cold water. When cold, dip in the yolk of well-beaten egg; then roll in bread or cracker crumbs highly seasoned. Put in pan with butter, a little veal or chicken stock. Bake a light brown. Add the juice of a lemon, or if preferred, a little sherry wine to gravy. Serve on toast.—Mrs. Penelope Barnett, Grantville, Ga.

Baked Calf's Head.—Wash the head well in cold water, crack the bones, and put into four quarts of cold water.

Set upon the back of the stove and let simmer for twenty-four hours. Take the head from the pot, place on a dish and carefully remove all the bone and the brains. Put the latter into a bowl and set aside for soup. Chop the meat rather fine, and season with a half teaspoon ground allspice; cayenne pepper and salt to taste. Put into a baking pan and set into the oven until nicely browned. Serve on a flat dish garnished with thin slices of lemon; pour over meat one or two wineglasses of good sherry and serve hot.—Mrs. Henry Boylston, Atlanta.

Coquille de Volaille.—Boil until tender, two chickens, then remove the rice and mince fine the white meat and place in a porcelain kettle with one tablespoon of chopped parsley, one and one-half tablespoons of butter, one can of mushrooms chopped fine, and one-half can truffles chopped very fine, (mushrooms and truffles should be tender), stir gently for thirty minutes, then add three-fourths of a pint of sweet cream, pepper and salt to your taste. When nearly ready to boil stir in one-half a teacup sweet cream (into which you have mixed two tablespoons of flour); this should thicken the coquille. But the art of making them a success is not to make them too dry nor too thin. Have ready one dozen silver or porcelain shells, fill with the coquille mixture; sprinkle over the top toasted bread crumbs. Put in the oven for ten minutes to brown. Serve very hot. As an entree, it is unsurpassed. A wineglass of sherry added just before placing in the shells is an improvement, but not a necessity.—Mrs. Jno. P. Richardson, New Orleans, La.

PICKLES.

Red Pepper Catsup.—One gallon vinegar, add eighty bell peppers, two tablespoons salt, two tablespoons mustard, three onions, handful horse-radish if you have it. Boil until the pulp slips from skin. When cold rub through sieve, bottle and seal it.—Mrs. M. J. Wisdom, Corinth, Ga.

Grape Catsup.—Five pounds grapes boiled and strained. Take two and one-half pints of sugar to one pint of vinegar, one tablespoon of cinnamon, one of cloves, one of allspice, one of pepper, one-half pound of salt. Boil until the catsup is thick. Put in bottles and seal.—Miss Anna Force, St. Louis, Mo.

Mango Pickle.—One peck of mangoes, after having been in brine. Remove all seed and soak for twenty-four hours, then put them on the fire in a little water and vinegar with one-half ounce of turmeric and one tablespoon of alum, and a few grape or fig leaves. Let come to a boil, then take off and stuff with a dressing made of a medium-size cabbage chopped fine, one-half dozen onions, one-half pound each of white and black mustard seed, one pound of brown sugar, two tablespoons of whole allspice, two of whole cloves, one of ground cinnamon, two of black pepper, two of celery seed, one-fourth pound of mustard, a little mace and a little horse-radish chopped fine; mix with a little vinegar. Fill the mangoes, put in jars and cover with good apple vinegar.—Mrs. R. M. Bell, Montgomery, Ala.

Tomato Catsup.—The tomatoes should be fully ripe and free from decay, scalded and pressed through a sieve. To one gallon of the juice, put one quart of sharp vinegar, four tablespoons of salt, four of black pepper, three of mustard, one of allspice, and four or five pods of red pepper. Slowly simmer in a preserving kettle, for three or four hours, occasionally stirring and skimming it. When cooked down quite thick, take out the red pepper, and it is ready for use. Bottle when cold.—Miss M. J. Green, Atlanta.

Chili Sauce.—One quart peeled, ripe tomatoes, two teacups sugar, five of vinegar, two of onions, three small pods of green peppers, with seed removed; chop all fine; two tablespoons of mixed spices, beaten fine. Mix and cook thick.—Mrs. R. L. Palmer, Atlanta.

Artichoke Pickles.—To one gallon best cider vinegar add three-fourths teacup white sugar, eight medium onions, cut fine, two cloves of garlic, cut fine, one-third teacup white ground pepper, two tablespoons of powdered horse-radish, two of celery seed, two of turmeric; salt to taste. Scrape artichokes well, and pour prepared vinegar over them. Tie up carefully.—Mrs. T. H. Bell, Atlanta.

Picklelily.—One peck small green tomatoes; slice and put them in salt for twenty-four hours. Then take one-fourth pound white mustard seed, four tablespoons of ground mustard, three of black pepper in grains, two ounces ground black pepper, one ounce cloves, one ounce mace, four nutmegs (pulverize large spices), twelve large onions sliced; put layers of tomatoes, onions and spices in kettle, cover with vinegar, and cook slowly for three hours. Stir constantly. —Mrs. W. A. Bass, Atlanta.

Sweet Pickled Beets.—Boil the beets in a porcelain kettle until tender, place them in cold water and remove the skin. Cut in any desirably shaped slices and put in glass jars. Make syrup of vinegar and sugar in proportion of one and one-half pint of sugar to one quart of vinegar, one teaspoon of ground cloves, tied in a cloth, pour boiling hot over beets and seal.—Mrs. S. K. Linscott, Holton, Kansas.

Green Pepper Mangoes.—Take the cap off the stem end of the pod with a pair of scissors; scrape out the seed. Lay the pods in weak salt and water for one hour. Take well-headed cabbage; chop very fine. To every quart add one tablespoon of salt, one of ground pepper, two of white mustard seed, one teaspoon of ground mustard. Mix this well. Chop fine a small quantity of horse-radish. Drain the peppers, stuff with the mixture, replace the caps and tie securely. Pack in jar with the small end down and pour over cold vinegar. Spices and sugar can be used if preferred. Will be ready for use in three weeks.—Mrs. Frank P. Rice, Atlanta.

Peach Mangoes.—Select firm, large peaches and with a sharp knife cut in half. Cut out the stone, replace the pieces and tie them together. Have ready a sufficient quantity of chopped cabbage and onions which has been covered with salt and water the day before. Throw the first into cold water and then season with white mustard and celery seed. Fill the peaches and tie them again. To one gallon of vinegar put three pounds of granulated sugar, spice to taste, two tablespooons of mustard which has been mixed with cold vinegar, and two of turmeric. When this is at boiling point throw in the fruit and allow it to remain five minutes. Put away in jars while hot.—Mrs. Wm. B. Lowe, Atlanta.

Pickled Figs.—Pick the figs with the stems on them when they are swelling to ripen. Soak ten or twelve hours in brine, get good apple vinegar, add three pounds of brown sugar to every gallon of vinegar, with such spices as you prefer, cloves, allspice, cinnamon and black pepper. Put the vinegar, spices and sugar on (sufficient vinegar to cover the figs) in a kettle and when it begins to simmer (wash the figs clean of all salt) put the figs in and let them get boiling hot, take them out and boil the vinegar down some, then pour over the figs boiling hot. They will be ready for use in eight days.—Miss Lucy Hatchett, Montgomery, Ala.

Chili Sauce.—Twenty-four ripe tomatoes, scald, skin and slice; also eight onions, six green peppers, eight tablespoons of salt, eight of sugar, one of cinnamon, one of allspice, one of nutmeg, one of cloves. When it has boiled three hours and is quite thick, add eight teacups of vinegar and one tablespoon of celery seed. Seal while hot.—Mrs. Mary R. K. Fowlkes, Selma, Ala.

Watermelon Rind Pickle.—After cutting the rind in any shape you fancy, soak twelve hours in lime water, made by dissolving two handfuls of lime in three gallons of water, change from bottom to top twice. Next scald in alum water. Then put in preserving kettle and cover with water, boil half an hour. Take out rind and plunge in cold water, repeating the process six times. Then boil in ginger tea half an hour. To make syrup—eight pounds of rind, five of sugar, three pints vinegar, two tablespoons of spice, one of mace and two of cinnamon. Put spices in muslin bag and boil with rind till tender. This is a splendid recipe and will repay for trouble.—Mrs. Daniel Chandler Jones, Atlanta.

Ax-Jar Pickles.—To each gallon of vinegar add one ounce nutmeg grated, one ounce mace, one ounce allspice, one ounce cloves, one ounce ginger, one ounce turmeric, one-half

MRS. ALBERT H. COX,
Auditor and Chairman Committee on Household Economics.

pound white sugar, one-third pound each of white and black mustard seed, one-fourth pound ground mustard in vinegar, one pint of rum, a little horse-radish grated. Keep jar well stirred; add a few garlic cloves sliced.—Mrs. J. K. Barnwell, McIntosh Co., Ga.

Spiced Apples.—Eight pounds apples peeled and cored, four pounds of sugar, one quart vinegar, one ounce stick cinnamon, one-half ounce whole cloves. Boil vinegar, sugar and spice together. While boiling add apples, a half at a time. Boil until tender. Twenty minutes will suffice. Remove and add others until all have been in the jar. Boil the syrup until thick as you like and pour over. Should there be too little to cover the fruit, sweeten and scald enough vinegar to thoroughly cover the apples. Cover the jar with a wax cloth.—Mrs. A. D. Adair, Atlanta.

VEGETABLES.

Time for Cooking Vegetables.—Green peas, one-half hour; parsnips, one hour; string beans, three hours; carrots, two hours; squash, one hour; beets, four hours; asparagus, twenty minutes; shelled beans, one hour; cabbage, two hours; onions, one hour; turnips, one and one-half hours; potatoes, one-half hour.

Macaroni with Tomatoes.—Boil one pound of macaroni in milk until tender (but not enough to break). Have ready one can of tomatoes hot, in which put one teaspoon of butter, a little salt, and red pepper. Take the macaroni while hot, pour in a deep dish, sprinkle grated cheese thickly over it, then turn the tomatoes over the cheese in the same dish.

You will find this a delightful dish to be eaten with crackers.—Miss Lula Belle Hemphill.

Green Corn Pudding.—Six ears of corn grated, one quart sweet milk, six eggs, one cup white sugar, one teaspoon lemon essence. Cream butter, sugar and yolk of eggs together; add milk, corn and essence. Last add the beaten whites of eggs. Bake in a moderately hot oven. Serve hot.—Miss Sallie Elkin, Lancaster, Ky.

Potato Puffs.—Boil and mash fine three Irish potatoes while warm; add one large tablespoon of lard, a coffee cup of sweet milk, in which dissolve half a cake of compressed yeast; mix in enough flour to make a soft dough; set to rise in a bowl well greased, and let stand until quite light; then sprinkle out about an inch thick, cut with a small biscuit-cutter, place them a little apart in the pan; let them rise again, then light bake in a quick oven.—Mrs. Judge James Jackson, Atlanta.

Parisian Stuffed Mushrooms.—If the mushrooms have not been cooked or canned, remove the stems, peel the cup, put in water and vinegar to soak. Boil stems in water and lemon juice, mash with small herbs and chicken, veal or pork. Put some bread crumbs in sweet milk, let soak, then squeeze out the milk and mix the bread with the hashed meat. Stuff the mushrooms with this mixture and serve with cream butter sauce —Mrs. Wm. M. Dickson, Atlanta.

Spaghetti.—One large onion sliced very thin, two small pieces of garlic cut very fine, two tablespoons flour, four of olive oil. Fry a light brown. Add gradually one large cup of stock, one quart can of tomatoes, a little parsley chopped fine, a little nutmeg, three whole cloves, salt and pepper, and one can of French mushrooms. Put in the entire contents of the can of mushrooms and cook three-fourths of an hour. Put spaghetti in boiling water, boil gently until tender. In three-fourths of an hour drain perfectly dry. Grate some cheese, which sprinkle on a platter, then a little sauce on the cheese, then the spaghetti. Alternate until you have used it all.—Mrs. E. H. Roberts, Atlanta.

Candied Potatoes.—Boil your sweet potatoes, then slice and put in layers in your baking pan. Add sugar, butter and seasoning to taste, and pour on a half cupful of boiling water before you place in the oven to brown.—Mrs. W. H. Felton, Cartersville, Ga.

Broiled Tomatoes.—Select large, smooth, ripe tomatoes; slice without peeling. Have the griddle hot and broil for a few minutes, turning once. Place on a heated dish, and sprinkle a little sugar and salt on each piece and pour over a small quantity of melted butter. Serve immediately with slices of crisp toast.—Mrs. A. J. West, Atlanta.

Tomato Jelly.—Strain in the juice of two cans of tomatoes. Dissolve one-half box gelatine in hot water; when cool pour in the juice of the tomatoes, seasoning with pepper and salt to taste. Pour in mold to stiffen. When firm turn out on a lettuce leaf and serve with mayonnaise dressing. The mold should be about the size of a cup and have just enough in it to look like half of a tomato.—Miss A. F. Jenckes, Atlanta.

Macaroni.—Beef round four pounds, suet one-half pound, onions one quart, tomatoes one-half can or one quart, butter (if desired) one-half pound, wine (if desired) small glass sherry (or goblet of claret), parmassone cheese one-half pound. Break suet in small pieces and put in large kettle; slice onions and fry brown, add butter. Take meat (which should be well skewered), and place in mixture, turning over and about till well browned. Add tomatoes, cover close and simmer slowly eight hours; remove meat and strain gravy through colander. Add wine. Boil two and one-half pounds smallest macaroni twenty minutes in plenty of salt water, strain through colander. Place in tureen, sprinkle with grated cheese, pour gravy over and mix well.—Mrs. E. A. Angier, Atlanta.

Potato Souffles.—Boil four good-sized potatoes, mash and pass through a sieve. Scald in a clean saucepan half teacup sweet milk and tablespoon of butter; add to the potato with a little salt and white pepper, and beat to a cream. Add one at a time the yolks of four eggs, beating thoroughly, drop a pinch of salt into the whites and beat them to a stiff froth. Add them to the mixture, beating as little as possible. Have ready a buttered baking dish large enough to let the souffle rise without running over; bake twenty minutes in a brisk oven. Serve at once in the dish it was baked in. It should be eaten with meats that have gravies.—Mrs. Wm. T. Wilson, Murfreesboro, Tenn.

Potato Souffles.—Bake the potatoes till done, then cut a piece off large enough to allow the inside scooped out; mix with a large piece of butter, cream, pepper, and salt. To every two potatoes one egg will be required. Mix the yolks well with the potatoes, whip the whites to a strong froth, and lightly stir in, then fill the skins, put them into the oven and bake a light brown. If properly made they are extremely light, and are always liked.—Mrs. M. J. Speer, Atlanta.

Vol au Vent of Asparagus.—Make a puff paste with ½ pound butter, 1 pound of flour, proceeding as usual; keep the pastry very cool always. Roll out an inch in thickness. May be made any shape. Cut around the pastry with a sharp knife wet in hot water, trace a small oval on the pastry an inch and a half from the edge and bake the *vol au vent* about thirty minutes in a hot oven. Should be a delicate brown. Have your asparagus stewed and seasoned with butter, cream, pepper and salt, and fill while hot. Serve with a cream sauce immediately.—Mrs. Joseph Thompson, Atlanta.

SALADS.

Columbian Salad Cream.—One-half pint thick sweet cream, 2 hard-boiled eggs, 1 tablespoon of vinegar, 1 lemon, 3 tablespoons Durkee's salad dressing, 1 pinch sugar, dry mustard and red pepper, each the size of an English pea, salt to taste, making the mixture when finished a little more salt than you would think necessary, so as to prevent having to use extra salt on all of the different articles dressed with the cream. This quantity is sufficient for five people. Make in a soup plate with wooden or silver spoon, rub smooth, and gradually moisten into a paste, with a few drops of the cream, the mustard, pepper and sugar; then add the Durkee's salad dressing, thoroughly mixing it all. To this add the yolks of the eggs which have been in another plate, rubbed perfectly smooth, removing any small pieces which cannot be mashed. Now, add the cream, stirring as little as can be to mix it in, being careful to move the spoon backward and forward, then crossways from each side, because a constant movement around one way has a tendency to cause cream to go to butter. Stir in the vinegar, then the strained lemon juice, and lastly the salt. Now slice the whites of the eggs into rings and drop in, and put the mixture on ice till wanted. This cream is a delightful adjunct to a picnic dinner, and is invaluable to a housekeeper because of its varied uses. For chicken salad, prepare your meat, add to it cut up celery and the heart of headed up lettuce, and put in the refrigerator; just before serving, toss the meat up with enough of the cream, and serve in lettuce leaves. With tomatoes, slice carefully of uniform thickness on a towel, place when drained, with a silver knife on a platter, and set directly on ice when wanted; serve in small sauce plates, with the cream put in before the tomatoes are put in. For sardines, on a long platter make cradles of two curled lettuce leaves, lay three sardines that have been rinsed off with vinegar in each cradle, pour over them some of the cream, and on the center of each put a thin slice of hard-boiled egg, just before serving. Canned turkey and fresh or pickled shrimp make a fine salad by adding to them a few chopped hard-boiled eggs, some lettuce heart and shredded celery, dressing with the cream, and setting on ice till wanted. The Columbian cream is a perfect dressing for chilled lettuce, and delightful lettuce sandwiches are made by dipping the leaves, which have been made brittle by contact with ice, in the thick cream, and placing between thin freshly cut home-made light bread; and lastly, in the absence of anything to dress with it, it has been pronounced "good enough" simply spread on home-made light bread.—Mrs. Richard Grubb, Darien, McIntosh County, Ga.

Stuffed Peppers.—Gather large bell peppers, open them at the sides, leaving the stems, but taking out all the seeds. Soak them in ice water two or three hours. Take a quart of shrimps, chop them up fine with bread crumbs, a tablespoon of butter, a cup of sweet milk; stuff the peppers with this mixture, then put in a pan and cook slowly.— Mrs. Robert Rutherford, Houston, Tex.

French Mayonnaise.—The yolks of 6 raw eggs—beat very light and add very slowly (drop by drop) a goblet of best olive oil, beat until it becomes as thick as mush; boil 6 eggs, mash the yolks and mix with a teacup of weak vinegar, an even tablespoon of mustard salt, one of red pepper, one of sugar, one of salt; mix all well together. Put on fire a clean skillet, melt a piece of butter size of walnut, pour into the pan all of the above (both raw and cooked egg mixture), and stirring carefully, let it come to a brisk boil, and thicken slightly. Remove and place in glass jar. —Mrs. H. C. White, Athens, Ga.

Chicken Salad Dressing.—Four eggs boiled hard, mash yolks fine, two teaspoons of mustard, a pinch of red pepper, a little piece of butter, 2 tablespoons of sweet oil; then stir. Mix 2 tablespoons of vinegar, last 2 spoons of cream; if sour just as good. Put in a cool place to get thicker.—Mrs. G. W. L. Powell, Atlanta.

Salad Dressing.—A most delicious salad dressing for lettuce and tomatoes.—2 eggs, 2 tablespoons of Durkee's salad dressing, 1 teaspoon of salt, 2 teaspoons of sugar, ½ glass of thick cream. Boil the eggs hard; take yolks and rub with 1 tablespoon of the Durkee's dressing until it is perfectly smooth, then add the salt, sugar, black pepper and the whites of the eggs finely chopped or mashed, then add the other tablespoon of Durkee's salad dressing, and lastly, the ½ glass of cream.—Mrs. W. R. Hammond, Atlanta.

Salad in Jelly.—First make the plain lemon jelly, not using quite the amount of sugar. Fill bottom of salad dish with a little of the jelly, and set on ice. When hard, set in the salad dish, on top of the jelly, a bowl large enough to hold the desired amount of salad, and fill bowl with ice; pour jelly around until almost reaching the top of bowl. When the jelly is hard remove ice from the bowl and fill with warm water for a moment only; then remove bowl from jelly, being careful not to break the jelly. Make any of the ordinary salads, such as chicken, veal, lobster, shrimp, or nice red tomatoes sliced with a little green, as celery, lettuce, etc., mixed through, here and there. Place salad in the space left in the jelly, and cover salad with remaining jelly. After it has become a little hard, set aside in ice box. When wanted set dish in warm water a moment and turn salad on a platter. Have a mayonnaise dressing ready to serve with salad. Remember in making this salad the bottom of dish will be the top, when turned out.—Adeline Miller, Atlanta.

Dressing for Meat or Fish Salads.—Beat the yolks of 4 eggs with 3 tablespoons of olive oil, thoroughly, then add 8 tablespoons of vinegar, 2 of French mustard, butter the size of a small egg, 2 teaspoons salt, 1 of ground pepper, 1 of sugar, 2 of celery seed. Put all of these ingredients in a

MRS. WILLIAM A. HEMPHILL,
Chairman Committee on Professional Work of Women.

double vessel and cook like custard. When it begins to thicken, stir in the whites of the 4 eggs beaten to a stiff froth. When cold and just before pouring over salad, add ½ teacup thick cream. Of course, if it is celery salad, or the celery stalk is used, omit the celery seed.—Mrs. Chas. A. Collier, Atlanta.

Mayonnaise Dressing.—To the yolk of 1 egg, add ¼ of a teaspoon of mustard and ½ teaspoon of salt. Stir with a fork till thoroughly mixed. Add a few drops of olive oil, and stir till it is all worked in, before adding more oil; continue to add oil, a little at a time; when it becomes too thick to mix easily, stir in a little vinegar, and proceed as before. The quantity of oil added may be gradually increased. If too much is added at a time, the mixture will look thin and curdle. If this occurs put the plate on the fire, and stir hard; if this does not "bring" back the only way is to begin again with fresh ingredients and after it is well started, stir in the old. Have the eggs and oil cold and with a little care it will not curdle. 1 egg will absorb about ½ pint of oil. When finished the dressing should be the color of boiled custard and much thicker. Be careful to keep in a cool place until ready to use.—Mrs. James O'Neill, Atlanta.

Tomato Salad (Cone Shaped).—Five crisp, curly lettuce leaves for the base. Then 3 slices of tomato, with a small lettuce leaf filled with mayonnaise dressing for the apex. This arranged on a small plate makes a very attractive appearance on the table and is very appetizing besides.—Mrs. S. K. Linscott, Holton, Kansas.

Salads.

Slaw.—To 1 beaten egg add 2 tablespoons of sugar, a level teaspoon of flour, a heaping one of mustard, a tablespoon of butter and a cup of vinegar. Put into a stew pan, and when hot, add 1 quart of finely-shredded cabbage, with a little salt sprinkled over it. Stew 5 minutes. To be eaten hot or cold.—Mrs. J. P. Thornton, LaGrange, Ga.

Asparagus Salad.—Peel the tops of 1 quart of asparagus, and boil in salt and water until thoroughly done. Put on ice until ready for use. Mix 3 tablespoonfuls of olive oil, 1 of vinegar, ¼ teaspoon of salt, one-tenth of pepper, and pour over asparagus just before serving. Garnish dish with curled parsley.—Mrs. Mary W. Johnson, Atlanta.

Shrimp Peppers.—Pick your shrimp after being boiled with salt. Two or three large spoons of pounded crackers or stale bread crumbs, a large spoon of butter, pepper, black and red, and a little nutmeg. Mix well together. Core as many bell peppers as your mixture will fill, wetting them well with juice squeezed from the heads of the shrimp, and wine. If your shrimp is not fresh boiled, or you use canned shrimp, you must use more butter and wine or they will be too dry. Just bake enough to thoroughly heat through.—Mrs. J. Gadsden King, Atlanta.

Creamy Omelet.—Beat the yolks of four eggs, just a little, with a silver spoon; for each egg add a tablespoon of cream; season lightly with salt and pepper; stir in the whites of the eggs, beaten less than for cake. Have the omelet pan clean, smooth and hot. Put in a generous tablespoon of butter, and just as soon as it melts (be careful not to scorch it), turn in the mixture and at once begin to shake the pan with regular motion. While the top is still soft and creamy set the pan in the baker (which should be hot) and remove when the omelet is golden brown. Roll out into a hot platter and serve at once. Garnish with parsley sprigs.—Mrs. Callie Lumpkin King, Marion, Ala.

Cheese Omelet.—One teacup of mush, 1 heaping cup of grated cheese, lump of butter the size of an egg, 6 or 8 eggs beaten separately, whites whipped to a stiff froth. Put the butter into the hot mush, then add cheese and mush to the yolks after being well beaten. Stir in the whites last. Bake quickly. Do not allow it to stand after baking.—Mrs. Sue B. Hudson, Columbus, Miss.

BREAD.

Economy is not stinginess, as so many people seem to think; but it is the art of utilizing all the scraps, odds and ends, and of buying what is needed and nothing more. One writer tells us that a "crust saved is a crust earned," and it should be printed on every bread jar.

Waffles.—One and one-half pints of buttermilk, ⅓ teacup corn meal, 1 teaspoon soda, 1½ teaspoon of salt, 3 eggs beaten separately, butter the size of an egg, flour enough to make a thin batter; cream butter and add salt, corn meal, milk, and flour. Beat well; then stir in lightly the yolks and whites. Just before baking, stir in the soda, dissolved in a tablespoon of warm water.—Mrs. Hugh T. Inman, Atlanta.

Cream Puffing.—One cup meal, 1½ cup cooked hominy, 1 cup milk, ½ cup boiling water, 1 tablespoon butter, 1 heaping teaspoon yeast powder, 3 eggs. Put into a bowl the butter, salt, meal, hominy and milk; mash fine and after beating a few minutes, stir in hot water; then add eggs and yeast powder and beat well. Bake in shallow pans.—Mrs. John W. Grant, Atlanta.

Cheese Sticks.—One pound flour, ½ pound butter, 1 cup cheese, ¾ teaspoon red pepper, 1 teaspoon salt. Cut the cheese into very thin slices, put into the flour with the salt and pepper, and chop with a knife until well mixed. Add enough cold water to make a rather stiff dough. Wash the butter and roll into the flour, making a smooth paste. Put on ice till very cold, roll very thin and cut in strips about 4 inches long and ½ inch wide.—Mrs. W. G. Raoul, Atlanta.

Tea Bread.—Three eggs beaten separately, 1 full pint of flour, 1 teacup of sweet milk, 1 teaspoon of Royal baking powder mixed in flour, 2 teaspoons of sugar, 1 tablespoon of butter. Melt butter and mix with sugar and milk, then stir in the flour and eggs. Bake in a hot oven.—Mrs. P. F. Williams, LaGrange, Ga.

Tomato Toast.—Put some canned tomatoes in a frying pan with a little butter and salt; cook lightly, strain, then pour over slices of buttered toast which have been softened with a little cream.—Mrs. W. C. Glenn, Atlanta.

Graham Flour Gems.—One egg, 1 pint of sweet milk, 1 pint of Graham flour. Beat the eggs thoroughly and mix with the milk. Beat this gradually, adding the flour in a half hour. Pinch of salt. Have well-buttered pans piping hot. Fill pans even full of batter and put in a hot oven. Bake quick.—Mrs. Preston Miller, Atlanta.

Tea Muffins.—Two eggs well beaten, 1 teacup lightly filled with flour, 1 dessert spoon of yeast powder, 1 teaspoon of sugar, a pinch of salt. Sift this into the eggs, 1 tablespoon of condensed milk in ½ cup of water. Mix into the flour 1 teaspoon of melted butter. Do not have the batter too stiff, pour in muffin pans very hot and well greased. Bake in a quick oven. The amount will make 8 or 10 muffins.—Mrs. Augusta Moore, Atlanta.

Dixie Waffles.—One pint buttermilk, 1 pint of flour, 1 egg, ½ cup melted lard, salt to taste. Break the egg into a bowl, beat very light with egg-whip, stir in the melted lard, then add the flour and milk alternately, beat thoroughly. Add cold water until a thin batter; now sift in 1 teaspoon of soda, and bake quickly in hot waffle irons, well greased the first time, not necessary afterwards.—Mrs. Alex. M. Wallace, Atlanta.

Nasturtium Sandwiches.—Cut some white or brown bread very thin, and spread with the most delicate fresh butter. Then pick some nasturtiums, choosing the youngest and most perfect in form and color. Separate the petals, lay them between 2 pieces of the wafered bread and butter, and add a sprinkling of salt and white pepper. The crimson petals should peep out between the edges of the bread.—Mrs. Dallas Albert, Pittsburg, Pa.

Non de Scripts.—Mix 1 pint of flour with the yolks of 6 eggs and a pinch of salt; work until the dough is perfectly smooth, roll out as thin as a wafer, and cut into 3-inch squares. Fold these squares together and slash up for 2 inches, then drop into boiling lard. They fry into all sorts of shapes and make a beautiful dish. Pile them on a platter or cake basket and sprinkle powdered sugar over them. —Mrs. A. W. Calhoun, Atlanta.

Bread.

Scotch Scones.—One quart flour, 1 teaspoon sugar, ½ teaspoon salt, 2 teaspoons baking powder, large tablespoon lard, 2 eggs, 1 pint sweet milk. Sift together flour, sugar, salt and yeast powders; rub the lard in cold; add a piece of butter the size of an egg, then add egg and milk. Mix in smooth dough to handle. Flour the board, turn out the dough, give it 1 or 2 quick kneadings to complete smoothness, roll it out an eighth of an inch in thickness, cut it squares not larger than a soda cracker, fold in half to form three-cornered pieces. Bake on hot griddle eight or ten minutes.—Mrs. S. A. Ferrell, LaGrange, Ga.

Cheese Fonder.—One cup of bread crumbs, 1 cup of grated cheese, 1 cup of sweet milk, flour, eggs beaten separately. Bake in a baking dish twenty minutes. Serve immediately.—Miss Lillie Orme, Atlanta.

Lunch Bread.—Six eggs beaten separately, 4 tablespoons of butter stirred into the sugar, 1 pint of flour, 2 teaspoons of yeast powder sifted in it, 1 gill of milk. Bake in a quick oven. Eat hot with butter.—Mrs. Wm. Rushton, Atlanta.

Sally Lunn.—Seven teacups of flour, 1 cup of new milk, 3 eggs beaten separately, 1 cup of yeast, 1 large tablespoon of sugar, 2 teaspoons salt, ½ cup butter. Make a soft dough. When well risen knead and make into two pieces like large biscuit, put into two round or square pans, leaving room to rise well. When light bake until well done. Split and butter, turning the inner side up.—Mrs. Hildreth Smith, Atlanta.

Muffins.—Two cups flour, 2 tablespoons lard, 2 tablespoons sugar, ½ tablespoon salt, 2 eggs, 2 teaspoons baking powder, 1 cup sweet milk. Beat the sugar and butter together.

Add to this the whites and yolks of eggs, beaten separately, until light; sift the flour, salt, and baking powder together; pour in on the mixture of sugar, butter and eggs. Mix very lightly, but do not stir. Add to the milk, mix in lightly, pour in greased muffin pans, bake about fifteen minutes. The delicacy of this muffin depends upon its lightness.—Mrs. Edward Herbert Barnes, Atlanta.

Zephyr Wafers.—One cup of flour, 1 cup of sweet milk, butter size of small egg, salt to suit taste. The batter must be smooth, and must be baked in zephyr wafer molds.—Mrs. J. G. Truitt, LaGrange, Ga.

Yeast Muffins.—One pint flour, 1 cup sweet milk, 1 tablespoon butter, 1 egg, ¼ yeast cake. Beat egg, sugar, and butter together; add flour gradually until it makes a stiff batter. Just before putting in muffin rings, stir in 1 teaspoon of soda. When made up about 5 P. M., will be ready for tea. Bake in a hot oven.—Mrs. F. M. Farley, Atlanta.

Split Rolls.—One quart of flour, 1 egg beaten with a tablespoon even full of sugar; dissolve ½ cake of compressed yeast in a tumbler of warm water, stir well and pour it to the egg; sift the flour into a tray. Rub 1 tablespoon of lard or butter into the flour; mix and work until the dough is smooth. Set in a warm place to rise. When light, work over, and roll about half inch thick, butter the top evenly, fold together and cut with ordinary biscuit cutter; place in buttered pan to rise half hour. Place them in pan so as not to touch each other. Bake quickly and serve hot.—Mrs. James R. DuBose, Asheville, N. C.

Sally Lunn.—Two eggs, 1 teacup of lukewarm milk, butter size of a hen's egg, teaspoon of salt, 2 teaspoons of sugar,

1 dessert spoon of potato yeast, heaping pint flour. Beat the eggs separately; stir the sugar well into the yolks; add the whites, then the milk, the butter melted and cooled, the yeast and flour. Set this to rise, in winter, at 10 o'clock for 7 o'clock tea. At 4 o'clock, put in a cake mold for a second rising. No additional flour is needed then. It should be a batter at first that will drop from your spoon about as hominy would. This baked as muffins is excellent. They require less time for a second rising.—Mrs. W. T. Newman, Atlanta.

Corn Bread.—Take about 2 teacups of hominy, and while hot mix with it 1 very large spoon of butter; beat 4 eggs very light, and stir them into the hominy; next add about 1 pint of milk, gradually stirred in, and lastly 1 pint of corn meal. The batter should be of the consistency of a rich boiled custard; if thicker, add a little more milk. Bake with a good deal of heat at the bottom of the oven, so as to allow it to rise. The pan in which it is baked ought to be a deep one, to allow space for rising. It has the appearance, when cooked, of a baked batter pudding, and when rich and well mixed, it has almost the delicacy of a baked custard.—Mrs. A. V. Heard, LaGrange, Ga.

Bops.—One pint of rice flour, 3 eggs, 1 spoon of butter, and ½ pint of milk. Mix and beat well, and bake like cake. It is a delightful breakfast bread.—Miss M. P. Green, Atlanta.

Rice Cakes.—6 eggs, 1 cup boiled rice, 1 pint sweet milk, 1 cup cold water, salt, flour to make a batter, 1 teaspoon of yeast powder.—Mrs. J. W. Fears, Atlanta.

Boston Corn Cakes.—Two cups of meal, 1 of flour, ⅔ of a cup of sugar, 2 eggs, 2 heaping teaspoons of baking pow-

MRS. HUGH HAGAN,
Chairman Committee on Ways and Means.

der, 2½ cups of milk, and a little salt. Bake in gem pans. —Mrs. Edward E. Sanger, Atlanta.

Sally Lunn.—Three eggs beaten well together, ¾ of a teacup of sugar, ¾ of a teacup of melted butter, flour to make real stiff batter, some thicker than cake batter, 4 tablespoons of sweet milk, 1½ spoons of baking powder (heaped). Bake in a slow oven. It does not take long to bake. Try it with a straw. Grease the pan well.—Miss Jennie Inman, Atlanta.

My Premium Crackers.—Two pints sifted flour, 1 tablespoon of lard, rubbed well together; make into a very stiff dough, with 1 teacup of cold water, in which has been dissolved 1 teaspoon of salt. Beat until smooth and divide into four equal parts; roll each piece until twelve inches square, cut into three-inch squares, stick with a fork; line the bottom of a pan with white paper, greased slightly. Put in the crackers and bake three or four minutes in a quick oven.—Miss Annie Dennis, Talbotton, Ga.

Sally Lunn.—Mix together 1 pint of sifted flour, 2 teaspoons of Royal baking powder, 2 tablespoons of sugar, ½ teaspoon of salt. Beat the yolks of 2 eggs; add to them ½ cup of sweet milk, measure scant ½ cup of butter. Put the two mixtures together, and lightly beating them with spoon, add the whites of the eggs beaten to stiff froth. Bake in hot oven twenty minutes.—Mrs. John W. Hurt, Atlanta.

Corn Meal Cakes.—One teacup sweet milk, 1 egg, 3 tablespoons of meal, and a little salt. The batter should be the consistency of cream. Bake on a very hot griddle.—Mrs. Maria Cole, Inman Park.

Bread.

Sally Lunn.—One quart flour, 1 egg, 1 yeast cake, lard size of small hen egg, dessert spoon of sugar. Beat the yolks of eggs with the sugar and lard; dissolve the yeast cake in ½ teacup of tepid water and add; then the sifted flour and 1 teaspoon of salt, and make a very stiff batter with a little lukewarm boiled milk. Set by the fire to rise. In three or four hours, work and make out in a pan, one layer at the bottom, greased with a little lard, and the other layer on top of that. Set to rise and then bake.—Mrs. A. H. Colquitt, Edgewood, Ga.

Beaten Biscuit.—One pound of flour, 4 ounces of lard, ½ teacup of sweet milk, 2 teaspoons of salt. If too stiff, add a little cold water. Beat until the dough is soft and blisters. Stick and cook.—Mrs. Bishop Paine, Aberdeen, Miss.

Gate City Corn Bread.—One and a half large cups corn meal, 3 large cups flour, ½ large cup butter, 1 large cup sugar, 1 pint milk, 2½ teaspoons baking powder.—Mrs. Charlie Tift, Albany, Ga.

Light Bread.—Boil 1 quart of morning's milk, remove from the fire and stir until lukewarm, add 1 tablespoon of fine salt and 2 tablespoons of sugar. Then add flour enough to make stiff batter. Put in a warm place until it rises. Add flour enough to make into a stiff dough. Let it rise again and bake brown.—Mrs. D. S. Porter, Flowery Branch, Ga.

Rice Bread.—Boil 1 pint of rice till soft, then mix it with 1 quart rice or wheat flour. When cool add ½ teacup of yeast, a little salt, and milk enough to make it of the consistency of light bread. Knead lightly.—Mrs. Abbie R. Hopkins, McIntosh Co., Ga.

CAKE.

General Hints.—The whites of eggs beat stiffer and much quicker when quite cool; therefore keep them on the ice until wanted for use. The nature of salt is cooling and all cakes that are composed largely of the whites of eggs should have a good pinch of salt added before beating. Do not mix up a cake in a bowl that has just come out of hot water; cool it with cold water. It will save you work in the end. The fresher the eggs the better the result in cake making. Stir butter and sugar to a cream. It will repay you to always use fresh butter. When fruit is used sprinkle with flour. Sift baking powder in the flour. Always dissolve your soda in milk. Beat whites and yolks separately. Try the recipes *as they are* first.

Dolly Varden Cake.—Four eggs, 2 cups white sugar, ½ cup butter. Beat hard half an hour, then add 3 cups flour, 1 cup sweet milk, 2 teaspoons of baking powder. Beat well together. Take out half the quantity, and add to it 1 cup of raisins, ½ cup of currants, ½ nutmeg, 2 teaspoons cinnamon, 2 of cloves. Bake the light and dark in separate pans 1 inch thick. Put icing between and pile them up.—Mrs. Benjamin F. Abbott, Atlanta.

Green Fruit Cake.—Take the whites of 15 eggs, 1 pound flour, 1 pound sugar, ½ pound butter, 3 teaspoons cream tartar, 1 teaspoon of soda, 1 tablespoon sweet milk, extract lemon. Sift cream tartar in flour; cream butter and flour well together. Beat whites of eggs and sugar together. Mix gradually so there will be no lumps. Add soda just before baking. Bake into one large cake. When thoroughly cold slice into six layers, spreading between icing, grated cocoanut, bananas sliced, Malaga grapes cut thin, pineapple. Ice on the outside, and while damp cover

over with cocoanut; trim with grapes and bananas.—Miss Annie Ligon, Columbus, Ga.

White Fruit Cake.—Sugar 1 pound, butter ¾ pound, eggs whites of 16, cocoanuts 2 large, almonds 1 pound, citron 2 pounds. Flour the fruit well so that it will not settle to the bottom of cake.—Mrs. M. A. Abrahams, LaGrange, Ga.

Black Fruit Cake.—One pound butter, 1 pound flour, 1 pound dark brown sugar, 2 eggs, 3 pounds seedless raisins, 1 pound currants, 1 pound citron, 1 ounce ground cinnamon, 1 ounce of spice, 1 ounce of cloves, 1 tumbler of wine, 1 tumbler of whisky, ¼ pound of dried figs.—Mrs. A. L. Hull, Athens, Ga.

Superior Sponge Cake.—Beat thoroughly the yolks of 6 eggs with 2 tablespoons of cold water; add slowly 2 cups of sugar, beating with egg-whip until frothy and white; then stir in the beaten whites of 6 eggs, 3 cups of sifted flour; lastly 2 teaspoons of baking powder dissolved in ½ cup of cold water. Flavor with lemon.—Mrs. John L. Cowles, Athens, Ga.

Tea Cakes.—Two pounds flour, 1 pound sugar, ½ pound of butter, ½ cup milk, 1 teaspoon of soda, 2 of cream tartar, 6 eggs. Knead the dough very soft.—Miss Jennie English, Atlanta.

Silver Cake.—Whites of 7 eggs, 1 cup butter, 2 cups sugar, 4 cups flour, 1 cup sweet milk, 2 teaspoons of baking powder. Cream butter and sugar, add the milk; then alternate with the flour and beaten whites of eggs. Sift the powder in the flour previous to mixing. Lemon Cheese Filling for Cake: Yolks of 3 eggs, juice and grated rind of

2 lemons, ¼ pound of butter, ½ pound of sugar. Put on fire and stir till cooked rather stiff, then stir in whites, beaten to a stiff froth; boil a few minutes, then take off and stir till cool. Use any cake batter preferred.—Mrs. W. C. King, Atlanta.

Black Fruit Cake.—Twelve eggs, 1 pound sugar, 1 pound flour, 1 pound of butter, 1 cup molasses, 1 tumbler of brandy, 1 teaspoon soda, 1 tablespoon of nutmeg, cinnamon, cloves, 1 teaspoon of allspice, 2 pounds raisins, 2 pounds currants, 1 pound citron, ¼ pound almonds, a few dates and figs; about 3 figs and ½ dozen dates. If you prefer, you can use more raisins and less currants. Flour the fruit well by using half the flour and about 1 ounce more. I brown half of my flour to make it black. Stir the soda in the molasses. Mix as you would in pound cake batter.—Mrs. Thomas Clarke, Atlanta.

Cake with Apple Filling.—Three eggs well beaten, 3 cups flour sifted with 2 teaspoons of baking powder, 1½ cups of white sugar, 1½ cups butter, ½ cup of sweet milk. Filling: 3 apples, ⅔ cup of sugar, 1 egg well beaten, juice and rind of 1 lemon. Mix all and stir constantly while cooking; then cool and place between layers of cake.—Mrs. Bulow Campbell, Atlanta.

Boiled Sugar Sponge Cake.—One pound sugar, ½ pound flour, 7 eggs, 1 tablespoon vanilla. Boil the sugar in 5 tablespoons of water for a few minutes. Beat the eggs separately. Sift the flour twice, first warming it slightly. Stir the mixture gently, adding the flour last. Bake twenty minutes.—Mrs. S. T. Davis, Federalsburg, Md.

Cake.

Tutti Frutti Cake.—Whites of 8 eggs, 2 cups sugar, 1 of butter, 3 full cups of flour, 1 of sweet milk, 3 teaspoons of baking powder. Bake in layers. Filling: Take ¼ pound of crystallized cherries, pineapple, English walnuts, any kind of fruit liked can be added. Cut fruit fine and put between layers after they are iced. Put English walnuts in halves all over top.—Mrs. J. D. Moreland, LaGrange, Ga.

Naples Drop Biscuit.—To 6 eggs well beaten add 1 pound of sugar, beat thoroughly, then stir in 1 pound of flour lightly, and flavor with lemon. Drop on buttered tins.—Mrs. Kate W. Cannon, Neosho, Mo.

Jam Cake.—(One of my favorite recipes.) Yolks of 8 eggs, 1 cup butter, 2 cups sugar, 3 cups flour, 1 cup jam, 1 cup wine, 2 heaping teaspoons baking powder, 1 teaspoon each of cloves, cinnamon, and mace. Sift baking powder in flour, beat eggs and sugar together until light, add butter well creamed, then the flour, spices, jam, and lastly the wine. Bake in layer pans, put together with icing. A fine substitute for fruit cake.—Mrs. N. P. Black, Atlanta.

Velvet Cake.—Take 1 cup of butter and 3 cups of sugar, cream until very light; then break 1 egg at a time and beat well until you have added 6 eggs. Add 3 cups of flour. Lastly add 1 teaspoon of soda dissolved in buttermilk. Flavor with vanilla.—Mrs. A. E. Grambling, Atlanta.

Chocolate Cake.—(Excellent.) For the Chocolate: ½ cake of Baker's chocolate (grated), 1 cup of white sugar, ½ cup of sweet milk, the yolks of 2 eggs. Mix well and boil until the sugar and chocolate are melted. Then set to cool and add 1 teaspoon of vanilla. For the Batter: 1 cup of white sugar, ½ cup of butter, ½ cup of sweet milk and the

yolks and whites of 2 eggs beaten separately. 2½ cups of flour and 1 teaspoon of soda dissolved in milk. Then add the boiled chocolate last. Bake in jelly cake pans. Icing: 2 cups of white sugar, ½ cup of water, and boil until it will harden in water; then stir this into whites of 2 eggs beaten stiff, stirring constantly. Flavor with vanilla.—Ellice Serena, Pittsburg, Pa.

Angel Food.—Whites of 11 eggs, 1½ cups of granulated sugar sifted, 1 cup of flour sifted seven times or more, 1 level teaspoon of cream tartar sifted with flour the last time. 2 teaspoons vanilla, a pinch of salt. Do not grease tins. Beat the whites to a stiff froth, add the sugar and beat five minutes with the Dover egg-beater; then take your spoon. Beat in the vanilla, salt, and flour last of all. Beat as little as possible, after adding flour. Pour in pan and bake in moderate oven one hour or until it leaves side of pan. Do not allow it to be jarred or shaken in the oven, or open the door for the first fifteen minutes, as much of the success of this delicious sweet depends upon the baking. When done, open the oven door and let it cool off gradually. After a few moments, if the pan has a tube, turn it upside down upon it, if not, rest it upside down upon two even supports. When cold, loosen from the sides of the tin with a sharp knife. Cover with boiled icing.—Mrs. Thomas H. Morgan, Atlanta.

White Cake.—Whites of 15 eggs, 1 pound flour, 1 pound sugar, ¾ pound butter. Cream butter and flour; beat eggs and sugar. After mixing, add 1 teacup of warm water and 1 teaspoon of baking powder. Flavor with vanilla.—Mrs. H. T. Phillips, Atlanta.

Cake.

Marsh Mallow Cake.—Whites 18 eggs, 2¼ cups pulverized sugar, 1½ cups flour, 2 teaspoons cream tartar, 1 teaspoon of vanilla. Beat eggs very light, then cut the sugar in with a broad blade carving knife. Sift flour three times with cream tartar in it, then cut in the egg and sugar, add vanilla. Bake in three layers. Don't grease the pans, put paper in bottom, have quick oven. Filling: 2 cups sugar boiled with 1 cup of water until syrup ropes. Just before taking off fire, add ½ pound marsh mallows broken in bits to melt partially. Pour the mixture gradually over the well-beaten whites of 2 eggs. Beat until cold. Put between cakes and on top very thick.—Mrs. Albert Cox, Atlanta.

Governor Northen Cake.—Whites of 8 eggs, 1 cup of sweet milk, 1 cup of butter, 2 cups of sugar, 2 cups of flour, 1 cup of corn starch, 2 tablespoons of Horsford's baking powder mixed with flour. Cream the butter and sugar, add the milk, flour, and corn starch, then the whites beaten very light. Bake in cakes about an inch thick. Icing for Same: Whites of 4 eggs beaten very light, 4 cups of sugar. Pour ½ pint of boiling water on the sugar; boil until clear and candy. Pour the boiling sugar over the beaten eggs and beat till cold, to a stiff cream. Before it is quite cold add 1 teaspoon of cream tartar, 2 teaspoons of vanilla. When cold, spread between the cakes as thick as the cake; also on top and sides.—Miss Zoe Brown, Sparta, Ga.

Filled Cake.—Seven heaping tablespoons butter, 6 heaping tablespoons of granulated sugar, 3 eggs, yolks and whites beaten separately. Just enough flour to make dough sufficiently stiff to mold with hands in the pan. Cream the

MRS. WILLIAM D. GRANT,
Chairman Committee on Patents and Inventions.

butter and sugar together, then beat in eggs, and lastly stir in flour, mixing it just enough to thoroughly incorporate it with the other ingredients. The less flour used the richer the cakes. Put a layer of dough about one-fourth inch thick in bottom of well-buttered square stove pan; then spread pineapple marmalade one-fourth inch thick over it, and over this another layer of dough of the same thickness. Stick the top layer closely with shredded citron and blanched almonds. I prefer making my own marmalade, as it is nicer than that offered for sale. Bake cake in moderately hot oven.—Mrs. C. A. Collier, Atlanta.

Japanese Cake.—One cup butter, 2 cups sugar, 3 cups flour, 4 eggs, 1 cup milk, 1 teaspoon of yeast powder. Divide this in half and bake two layers of plain batter. Into the other half put teaspoon each of cloves, cinnamon and spice, and ¼ pound of raisins chopped fine, and bake two layers of this. Spread between each layer a mixture made as follows: Juice and grated rind of 2 lemons, 1 cocoanut, 2 cups sugar, and 1 cup of boiling water. When this begins to boil, add 1 tablespoon of corn starch, and cook till it drops in lumps from spoon.—Mrs. Young J. Allen, Shanghai, China.

Five O'clock Tea Cakes.—Three-fourths pound sugar, ½ pound flour, ½ goblet of ice water, 7 eggs, 1 teaspoon vanilla, ½ teaspoon baking powder. Bake in 2 square shallow pans in a quick oven. Turn them out, put a layer of icing between, and with a sharp knife cut them into cubes. This quantity makes 3 dozen. Ice them with a firm boiled icing, and when cold and dry, tie with narrow ribbons to match the color scheme of the entertainment. These cakes are not only good to eat, but a basket of them adds greatly to the beauty of a table.—Mrs. Geo. A. Speer, LaGrange, Ga.

Ginger Wafers.—Two cups flour, 1 cup brown sugar, 1 cup butter, 1 cup sweet milk, 1 tablespoon ginger. Roll very thin and bake.—Mrs. Wm. Lawson Peel, Atlanta.

Ginger Cake.—One cup butter, 1 cup brown sugar, 1½ cups black molasses, 3 cups of flour, 5 eggs, ½ cup ginger, ½ teaspoon soda, ½ cup sweet milk.—Mrs. Caroline Bleckley, Atlanta.

Chocolate Wafers.—One cup brown sugar, 1 cup of granulated sugar, 1 cup of butter, 1 egg, 1 cup of grated chocolate, 1 teaspoon vanilla, enough flour to make stiff (about 1½ cups). Roll very thin, cut with square cutter or tin lid. Bake quickly. Very nice for afternoon receptions.—Mrs. Salouel McKinley Bussey, Atlanta.

Mother's Jumbles.—Yolks of 12 eggs, 1 pound of sugar, ½ pound of butter, ½ teacup of cream, 1 teaspoon of soda. Mix very soft. Roll thin, season with cinnamon and nutmeg. Sprinkle sugar over top before baking. A nice way to use the yellows after making white cake.—Mrs. R. C. Clarke, Atlanta.

White Cake.—Four cups of flour, 3 cups of sugar, 1 cup of butter, 1 cup of milk, whites of 7 eggs, 1 teaspoon soda, 2 teaspoons of cream tartar. For fruit cake, add 1 package dessicated cocoanut, 1 pound citron, 1½ pounds almonds, mace to taste.—Mrs. Miriam Lumpkin Nichols, Atlanta.

White Cake.—Cream a heaping tablespoon of butter and 2 teacups of sugar together. Add alternately 1 cup of sweet milk, 4 cups of sifted flour and the whites of 4 eggs, well beaten. Lastly, 1 teaspoon of yeast powder.—Mrs. Robert A. Hemphill, Atlanta.

Raisin Cake.—One pound sugar, 1 pound flour, ¾ pound butter, 4 eggs, 1 pound raisins (after seeding), 1 cup buttermilk, ½ teaspoon soda, 1 glass wine. Mix in 1 teaspoon cinnamon, ½ of cloves, ½ nutmeg. Cream butter and sugar together. Beat eggs well, mix all. Bake four hours.—Mrs. Columbus A. Pitts, Atlanta.

Feather Cake.—Two cups sugar, 1 cup milk, ½ cup butter, 3 of flour, 3 eggs, 2 teaspoons of baking powder.—Mrs. John M. Billups, Columbus, Miss.

Almond Cream Cake.—Ten eggs, whites and yolks beaten separately, 1½ cups of pulverized sugar, 1 cup of cracker dust. Boss lunch biscuit beaten to powder and sifted are best. 1 pound of almonds in shell. Hull and beat without blanching, not too fine. Mix almonds with cracker dust, juice and rind of 1 lemon, 2 teaspoons of vanilla. Beat whites well. Beat yolks and sugar together. Add whites, then almonds and crackers alternately. Bake in layers and spread whipped cream between. To pint of cream whipped with a fork until thick like butter, add ½ cup of sugar, a little at a time. This quantity of cream will fill the top and layers. Cream must be thick. The almonds must not be finer than rice grains.—Mrs. H. A. Tarver, Albany, Ga.

Brownstone Front.—One and one-half pounds of icing (pulverized sugar), whites of 6 eggs, 1 teaspoon of vanilla. Make icing first and put in a cool place until cake is ready. Do not cook, only beat and spread on while cake is hot. Cake: 3 eggs, 2 cups of flour, 1 cup of sugar, ½ cup of butter, ½ cup of milk, 2 teaspoons of baking powder. Mix the above and add the following ingredients after they are mixed: 7 squares of Baker's chocolate melted over pan of hot water, 1 cup of sugar, ¾ cup of milk, yolk of 1 egg. Bake in jelly cake pans. The thinner the layers the better the cake.—Mrs. Samuel Martin Inman, Atlanta.

Texas Cake.—Five cups of flour, 3 cups of sugar, 1 cup of butter, 1 cup of sweet milk, whites of 1 dozen eggs, 2 teaspoons of cream of tartar, 1 teaspoon of soda.

Gold Cake.—Yolks of 1 dozen eggs, 4 cups of flour, 2 cups of sugar, 1 cup of butter, 1 cup of buttermilk, 1 teaspoon of soda, 1 teaspoon of cream of tartar.—Mrs. Nat Hammond, Atlanta.

Jumbles.—One pound butter, 1½ pounds of sugar, 8 eggs. leaving out the whites of 4, 2 pounds of flour, rose water, mace or nutmeg. Roll them in grated sugar; bake in a quick oven.—Mrs. Colin Frasier, Inman Park.

Sponge Cake.—Six eggs, leave out whites of 3, 2½ cups flour, 2 cups sugar, 1 cup boiling water, 1 tablespoon baking powder, a pinch of salt, juice 1 green lemon. Beat yolks of eggs and sugar until very light; then add the whites of 3 eggs beaten light; then boiling water; then the flour, warmed and sifted several times, and the baking powder sifted in the flour at the last. Frosting: 1 pound of pulverized sugar, ½ teacup boiling water, the whites of 3 eggs. Boil the sugar until it ropes from the spoon, then pour in a thin stream on the stiff beaten whites. Flavor. Make as layer cake, the icing between and on top.—Mrs. Mary R. K. Fowlkes, Selma, Ala.

Cake.

Washington Cake.—One-half pound of flour, ½ pound of sugar, ¼ pound of butter, ¼ pound raisins, ¼ pound of citron, ¼ pound of currants, 3 eggs, 1 cup of milk, 1 small teaspoon of soda, cinnamon and nutmeg to the taste, glass of wine and brandy mixed. Caramel Filling: 2 teacups of white sugar (granulated), lump of butter size of an egg, ⅔ cup of rich milk or cream. Put it in a stewpan on the back of stove to boil slowly. Put another cup of white sugar in a dry tin pan on stove and brown.—Mrs. Hattie Gould Jefferies, Augusta, Ga.

Doughnuts.—One cup sugar, 1 cup buttermilk, 1 teaspoon soda, 1 tablespoon butter, 1 egg, pinch salt, nutmeg, and flour enough to roll out soft.—Mrs. Dr. Sid. Holland, Atlanta.

Fruit Cake.—Five cups of sugar, (the brown sugar is the best), 1 pound of butter, 12 eggs, 6 cups of flour, 1 teaspoon of soda, 1 cup of strong coffee, 2 tablespoons of fine ground coffee, ½ glass of brandy or whisky, 1 pound almonds cut fine, 1 pound of Brazil nuts cut fine, 1 pound hickory nuts, 4 pounds raisins, 1 pound of citron, 1 pound of prunes cooked until soft, then chop, 1 cup of wine.—Mrs. W. H. Gainde, Montgomery, Ala.

Layer White Fruit Cake.—Take any nice batter and bake in jelly pans, then make an icing, and when well beaten, mix in to it ½ pound crystallized pineapple, ½ pound cherries, ½ pound of almonds. Cut all up in small pieces, then spread on the cake and over that sprinkle grated cocoanut. It is very nice.—Mrs. St. Julian Ravenell, Atlanta.

Premium Cake.[*]—Whites of 17 eggs, 3 cups of sugar, 3 cups of flour, 3 heaping teaspoons of cream tartar. Sift

---
[*] Has taken first premium at several Kentucky fairs.

sugar in eggs (well beaten), also cream tartar into flour. Mix well, stirring as lightly as possible. Flavor with lemon. Bake in four layers and ice together.—Mrs. J. R. McDowell, Lexington, Ky.

Black Caramel Cake.—Two cups brown sugar, 4 cups flour, 1 cup of butter, 1 cup of jam, 2 cups of raisins cut fine, 6 eggs, 2 heaping teaspoons of baking powder, 1 tablespoon of allspice, nutmeg and brandy to taste. Bake in three layers. Filling for Same: 3 cups brown sugar, 1½ cups of cream, 3 tablespoons of butter.—Miss Mary Harrison, Lexington, Ky.

Tea Cake.—Two cups of sugar, 1 cup of water, butter size of a walnut. Put in a pan on the fire and let boil until nearly a syrup, then add ½ cup of sweet milk; let boil little while longer until as thick as sauce. Take off and let cool. Have 3 eggs well beaten and beat them into the syrup and butter. Flavor this with nutmeg. Have in your tray 1 quart of flour. Mix in 2 large spoons of baking powder, ½ cup melted lard. Pour mixture into this and work into light dough, not stiff. Roll out; bake in hot oven.—Mrs. Wm. King, Atlanta.

Rocky Mountain Cake.—Make three layer cakes. Let one be a silver white and one a dark spice, and color one rosy pink. Grate 2 cocoanuts. Break into small pieces ½ pound of English walnuts and ½ pound of almonds. Cut up fine 1 pound of raisins and 1 pound of citron. Wash and pick ½ pound of currants. Make a good boiled icing. Place your first cake, and spread your icing on rather thin; sprinkle a thick layer of cocoanut, raisins, citron, and currants, and before putting on the next cake, ice the bottom side of this cake so it will stick to the layer of fruits and nuts. After it is all stacked, cover the whole with icing, sprinkle with cocoanut, and dot with the fruits and nuts. You will find this cake, served with a cup of hot chocolate, a dainty little repast in itself.—Miss Mamie O. Norris, Cartersville, Ga.

Crullers.—Ten tablespoons of sugar, 6 tablespoons of melted butter, 1 teaspoon of soda, 4 eggs well beaten, 1 cup sour milk, enough flour to roll into a soft dough, cinnamon, and nutmeg. Fry in boiling hot lard.—Miss Anita Black, Atlanta.

Spice Cake.—One cup of sugar, 1 cup of molasses, 1 cup of butter, 1 cup of sour milk, a little more than a cup of flour, 3 eggs, 1 large teaspoon of all spice except cloves, of that a scant teaspoon. To cup of sour milk add teaspoon soda, to cup of molasses add ⅔ teaspoon soda. Mix butter and sugar together, add eggs, then milk and molasses, and sift the soda in the flour. Boil the sugar for frosting until it ropes and to this add the well-beaten white of an egg. Between first and second layers put finely-chopped raisins with a little of the frosting. Use frosting alone on the top. —Mrs. B. W. Wrenn, Atlanta.

Cream Cakes.—One cup hot water, ½ teaspoon salt, ½ cup butter, 1½ cups pastry flour, 5 eggs, yolks and whites beaten separately. Boil the water, butter and salt. While boiling add the dry flour, stir well for five minutes, and when cool add the eggs. As this is such a stiff mixture some prefer to mix with the hand, and some rather add the eggs whole, one at a time. When thoroughly mixed, drop in tablespoonfuls on a buttered baking pan, some distance apart. Bake twenty or thirty minutes, or till brown and well puffed. Split when cool and fill with cream. Eclair: Bake the cream cake mixture in pieces four inches long and half that width. When cool split and fill with cream. Ice with chocolate or vanilla frosting.—Mrs. Moreland Speer, Atlanta.

Sweet Wafers.—Three eggs, their weight in flour and sugar, not quite their weight in butter. Stir as little as possible. Fry in wafer irons.—Miss Eugenia Rucker, Atlanta.

An Economical Cake.—Whites 6 eggs, 1 cup butter, 1 cup milk, 2 cups of sugar, 3 cups flour, 1 level teaspoon baking powder, 1 teaspoon vanilla. Cream well the butter and sugar; add the whites of 6 eggs beaten stiff. Add flour well sifted with baking powder, then add milk and beat till light and smooth. If, after mixing the ingredients, the batter is too soft, add enough flour to make it moderately stiff.—Miss Sally May Akin, Cartersville, Ga.

Hot Chocolate Cake.—One cup sugar, ½ cup butter, ½ cup sweet milk, 2 cups of flour, 2 eggs, 1 small teaspoon soda. Then add to ½ cup sweet milk 2 squares Baker's chocolate, grated. Put on to boil. Before taking off, add yolk of 1 egg, ½ cup sugar, 1 teaspoon vanilla. Stir this well while it is hot into the above cake batter. Bake in layers. Frosting to Put Between Layers: 1 cup sugar, ½ cup sweet milk, ½ square chocolate. Boil five minutes, then stir until cool and thick enough to spread between layers.—Mrs. Robert Winship, Inman Park.

Cream Cake.—Three eggs, 2 cups of sugar, ½ cup butter, 1 cup sweet milk, 3 cups sifted flour, 2 teaspoons of baking powder. To be eaten with sauce.—Miss Sallie Malone, Atlanta.

MRS. PORTER KING,
Chairman Committee on Library.

White Cake.—Cream 2 cups of white sugar with ¾ of a cup of butter. Add alternately 4 cups of sifted flour and the beaten whites of 10 eggs, then 2 teaspoons of baking powder dissolved in ½ cup of sweet milk. Flavor with lemon or rose.—Mrs. Sam. Jones, Cartersville, Ga.

Fig Cake.—Two cups of sugar, 1 cup of butter, 1 cup of milk, 8 eggs (whites only), 3¼ cups of flour, 2 teaspoons of baking powder, 1 pound of figs. Cut the figs in small slices, flour them, and mix in the cake when it is ready to bake. Bake in a slow oven, and make one large loaf.—Mrs. J. J. Duffy, Atlanta.

Lemon Sponge Cake.—Twelve eggs, beaten separately and well, 15 ounces of white sugar, ¾ pound of sifted flour, juice of 1 fresh lemon. Weigh 1 pound of sugar and take out 2 tablespoons, which will leave 15 ounces.—Mrs. Hugh McKee, Atlanta.

Crullers.—Six heaping tablespoons of sugar, 4 tablespoons milk or water, 4 tablespoons melted lard, 4 eggs, 1 nutmeg, 1 teaspoon soda. Dissolve the soda in the water or milk; knead in sufficient flour to prevent sticking. Cut in shapes and fry in boiling lard.—Mrs. G. A. Nicholson, Atlanta.

Butternut Cake.—One cup butter, 2 cups sugar, 1 cup milk, 3 cups flour, the whites of 5 eggs, 2 teaspoons baking powder, flavor to taste. Bake like jelly cake in three parts. In the middle layer stir in 1 cup of butternut meats. Place one over the other when baked, the middle layer having the nuts.—Miss Bessie Boyd, East Point, Ga.

Corn Pone.—One teacup of molasses, 1 tablespoon of salt, 3 pints warm water, corn meal. Sift the corn meal into a mixing bowl. Pour in the salt, molasses and water mix thoroughly, not too stiff. Let it stand in a warm place for five hours, then bake slowly for three hours.—Miss Sallie E. Norton, Norton, Ga.

Cocoanut Cake.—Whites of 8 eggs, yolks of 4, ½ pound butter, 1 pound of sugar, 1 pound of flour, 1 heaping teaspoon of yeast powders, 1 cup sweet milk. Beat the eggs separately, sift yeast powders with flour. Beat butter and sugar together, add milk last. Make 1 pound boiled icing. Take about half the icing and mix the cocoanut and spread between the layers of cake which have been baked in jelly pans. Flavor it with vanilla.—Mrs. Thomas Hardeman, Oxford, Ga.

Marsh Mallow Cake.—Five ounces gum arabic, cover with 8 tablespoons of warm water. Set aside for an hour, then put this over the teakettle and in a farina boiler. Stir constantly until the gum is dissolved. Strain it through a fine sieve or piece of cheese cloth; add to 7 ounces of powdered sugar (this will be little less than a cup). Stir until the sugar is dissolved. Beat the whites of 4 eggs to a stiff froth, and pour in the gum while hot. Beat about two minutes, add 1 teaspoon vanilla, and put aside until cold and stiff. Let the cakes be cold before you put the mixture between. Any white cake will do for the layers.—Mrs. A. W. Force, Atlanta.

Ginger Snaps.—One teacup of molasses, 1 cup brown sugar, 1 cup of butter and lard mixed, 2 eggs, 2 tablespoons of soda in ½ cup of boiling water, 1 good tablespoon of ground ginger, flour enough to make stiff dough. Roll thin and bake quickly.—Mrs. Wm. Drake, Atlanta.

Almond Cream Cake.—Two cups of sugar, ¼ cup of butter, 1 cup of milk, 3 cups of flour, 4 eggs (whites only), 3 teaspoons of baking powder, ½ teaspoon of vanilla. Bake in three layers. Filling: One cup of rich cream, whipped (to be measured before it is whipped), ½ cup of powdered sugar, 1 pound of almonds blanched and pounded to a paste, a few drops of vanilla. Spread thickly between layers, and ice the top and sides.—Mrs. H. R. Slack, LaGrange, Ga.

Sponge Cake.—This recipe never fails: Ten eggs, 1 pound sugar, ½ pound flour, 1 lemon; separate eggs, stirring yolks and whipping whites the same length of time, until whites are firmly foamed, adding the pound of sugar before the active stirring of yolks begins, also the juice of a large lemon and the grated rind; gradually adding the sifted flour, which must be stirred in lightly, and immediately turned in a papered pan and baked slowly.—Mrs. Charles Price, Salisbury, N. C.

PUDDINGS AND CUSTARDS.

Boiled Plum Pudding.—One pound butter, 4 pints of flour, 12 eggs, 1 quart of milk, 1 tumbler of whisky, 1 pound of sweet raisins, 1 teaspoon of soda. Cream butter and flour. Beat eggs separately. Add the whites last. Flour the raisins, and after mixing flour, butter, eggs, milk, and soda, lightly stir in the raisins. Flour a canton flannel bag, and pour in the mixture. Put the bag in a pot of boiling water; be careful not to let it touch the sides. Boil six hours, and serve with hard butter sauce.—Mrs. Gen. T. R. R. Cobb, Athens, Ga.

Puddings and Custards.

Delicate and Simple Dessert.—Bring to boiling point 1 quart of sweet milk. Add 6 tablespoons of sugar, then the beaten yolks of 4 eggs, stirring all the time until it thickens. Before boiling the milk, have ready 1 tablespoon of corn starch or 2 tablespoons of grated chocolate well dissolved in a little milk. Add this last. When cooked will be thicker than boiled custard. Flavor with 1 teaspoon of lemon and 1 of vanilla and pour in a pudding dish. Whip whites of eggs, beaten stiff, with 3 tablespoons of sugar. Return to oven and brown slightly. Serve with or without cake This is a nice dessert for Sunday as it can be made on Saturday. Always serve cold.—Mrs. Chas. Lovelace, Columbus, Ga.

Cottage Pudding.—One cup sugar, 1 sweet milk, 1 pint flour, 2 tablespoons melted butter, 1 teaspoon of soda, 2 of cream tartar, and 1 egg.—Mrs. Wm. J. Speer, Atlanta.

Green Tomato Pie.—For one pie, peel and slice 5 green tomatoes. Add 4 tablespoons of vinegar, 1 tablespoon of butter, 3 tablespoons of sugar. Flavor with nutmeg or cinnamon. Bake with two crusts slowly.—Mrs. A. A. Harmon, Atlanta.

Dixie Pudding.—One cup of sugar, 1 cup of bread crumbs grated fine, 3 eggs, 2 tablespoons of butter, 1 cup of figs or peach preserves, milk enough to make about the consistency of rice pudding. Pour into a pudding bowl and bake. Serve with a sauce.—Mrs. Dr. Richard L. Sykes, Columbus, Miss.

Plum Pudding.—(Simple but very good). One and one-half pints of grated bread crumbs (soft, not dried), 1 pint chopped suet, 1½ pints of currants and stoned raisins mixed, ½ cup of citron shaved thin, 1 scant cup of sugar, ½ teaspoon of salt,

½ teaspoon grated nutmeg, 5 eggs, 2 even tablespoons of flour made into a thin batter with milk and ½ glass of brandy. Mix in the order given. Boil or steam four hours. Serve with sauce.—Mrs. Louis Gholstin, Atlanta.

Chocolate Pudding.—The yolks of 6 eggs, 1¾ cups sugar, 1 cup cracker dust, 1 cup grated chocolate, then add whites beaten stiff. Bake. Eat with sauce.

Lemon Sauce.—One pound sugar, 3 ounces butter, ½ cup water, rind of 2 lemons, 2 teaspoons extract of lemon. Pour in saucepan, and when it comes to a boil, beat in the yolks of 2 eggs. When boiled, take it off from the fire. Add the 2 whites. Let boil a few minutes.—Mrs. Julius Alexander, Atlanta.

White Sauce.—Whites of 2 unbeaten eggs and 1 cup of sugar beaten together. Add 1 teaspoon of good vinegar; beat well, then add 3 tablespoons of good wine, and just as it goes to the table, add ⅔ of a cup of beaten (not whipped) cream.—Mrs. John Keely, Atlanta.

1 pound strawberries, ½ pound white sugar steamed twenty minutes in double kettle. 1 pound of plums, halved and stoned, 1 pound sugar; place in alternate layers in stone jar. Let them so remain for at least forty-eight hours; then boil twenty minutes.—Mrs. Wm. M. Darlington, Pittsburg, Pa.

White Custard.—One and one-half pints of cream, scalding hot. While the cream is heating, put the whites of 4 eggs in a bowl with 4 heaping tablespoons of sugar and 1 teaspoon of vanilla. Pour the hot cream on the eggs and sugar, stirring all the time. Put the custard in cups, set them in a pan of hot water, cover with a paper and bake until like jelly. Do not beat the whites of the eggs, or it will be spoiled.—Mrs. John Neal, Atlanta.

Citron Pudding.—Make pastry as for pies. ½ pound of butter, 1 pound sugar, 1 lemon, yolks of 12 eggs, citron. Cream butter and sugar; add yolks of 12 eggs, well beaten; then one or more lemons to taste; then add small, thin slices of citron on top. This will make two pies.— Mrs. Henry H. Inman, Atlanta.

Macaroon Pudding.—Let 1 quart of milk come to a boil, then stir in the yolks of 4 eggs, 1 cup of sugar, well beaten together. Soak ¾ of a box of Cox's gelatine in a cup of water and add to the custard. Let it come to a boil, take it from the fire and add the whites of the eggs, which must be beaten stiff. Fill a glass bowl about half full of macaroons, first dipping them in sherry wine, then pour over custard. Serve with whipped cream flavored with wine. —Mrs. James Scrutchens, Atlanta.

Date Mush.—One cup farina, ½ pound dates. Boil farina, and pour in small molds over cut up fruit. Serve cold with custard.—Miss Kitty Peters, Atlanta.

"1776" Mince Meat.—One tongue parboiled, the weight of it in suet and ½ pound more, all chopped fine, 2 pounds currants, 1½ pounds raisins stoned, 1 pound citron, 12 tart apples, ¼ ounce each cinnamon, cloves and nutmeg, juice 4 lemons, peel of 2 lemons chopped fine, ½ pint wine, 1½ pints brandy, 1½ pounds sugar, and some salt. Add juice of 2 more lemons if needed.—English, and owned by Richard Peters' family.

Golden Pudding.—Boil 1 quart of sweet milk, and add 5 tablespoons of flour, a little salt, 7 eggs (reserving whites of 3), 8½ cups sugar. Bake half hour.

Silver Sauce.—Whites of 3 eggs, beaten with 1½ cups of sugar, and a glass of wine. More wine improves the same. It is not so thick.—Mrs. Will Inman, Atlanta.

Temperance Mince Meat.—Two pounds chopped meat, the same of suet chopped fine, 2 pounds each of raisins and currants, ¾ pound of citron, 4 pounds chopped apples, 3 pounds sugar, and a pinch of salt. The juice of 4 oranges and a strong lemonade made of 6 lemons to stir into the mixture; spices to taste. Put above in a porcelain kettle and boil gently until the suet and apples are entirely dissolved; put in jars.—Mrs. W. H. Nutting, Atlanta.

Confectioners' Pastry.—One and one-half pounds of flour to 1 pound of butter. Mix a stiff dough with 1 tablespoon of lard and 1 of butter, add a little salt. Roll the dough and spread butter on it a number of times, until all of the butter is used.—Mrs. Harriet Gould, Augusta, Ga.

Lemon Meringue Pie.—Two large lemons, juice and rind, 2 teacups of sugar, 1 teacup of milk, 2 tablespoons of corn starch dissolved in the milk and poured in lastly, yolks of 6 eggs. Make a pie crust, fill with the above, and bake as a pie. Whisk the whites of eggs; add to them 8 tablespoons of powdered sugar; flavor with rose water. When the pie is baked, pour this mixture over it; set back in the oven until it becomes a delicate brown. The above makes two pies. A delicate bonne-bouché.—Mrs. L. B. Purnell, Baltimore, Md.

Ginger Pudding.—Two cups of syrup, 1 tablespoon of soda. Beat soda and syrup together, add 4 cups of sifted flour. ½ cup of sifted meal, 1 cup of buttermilk, 1 tablespoon of melted lard, 1 teaspoon of ginger. Bake in hot oven.—Mrs. Dr. Gillespie, Atlanta.

Lemon Pudding.—Six eggs, 2 cups sugar, 1 cup milk, 2 tablespoons corn starch, 2 lemons, rind of one, juice of 2; whites with 8 tablespoons of pulverized sugar.—Mrs. J. G. Armstrong, Atlanta.

Strawberry Short Cake.—One pint of flour, yolk of 1 egg, 1 tablespoon of butter, 2 tablespoons of sugar, 1 teaspoon yeast powder. Mix with sweet milk a soft dough. Bake, and while hot split and butter and put a layer of fresh strawberries well sweetened between the layers, one layer on top. Then cover with whipped cream, sweetened.—Mrs. Francis Fontaine, Atlanta.

Vevey Pudding.—¼ pound of rice, 1½ pints of rich milk, ⅛ box of gelatine, 1 teacup of white sugar, 1 pint of cream, 1 tablespoon of vanilla, 1 wineglass of sherry. Boil the rice in the 1½ pints of milk until very soft. Add the teacup of sugar, ½ teaspoon of salt, vanilla and wine. Dissolve the gelatine in as little water as possible and add to the pint of cream. Mix all together and pour into mold and set on ice. To be served with cream.—Mrs. Dr. Hunter P. Cooper, Atlanta.

Orange Pie.—Two cups of sugar, 3 cups of flour, 1 cup of milk, 3 eggs, 2 teaspoons of baking powder. Bake in Washington pie shallow tins. Filling: 2½ cups of water, 3 tablespoons of corn starch, grated rind of 2 oranges and juice of 3 oranges and pieces of 1 lemon, 1 cup of powdered

MRS. RHODE HILL,
Member Board of Women Managers.

sugar, 1 tablespoon of butter, and yolks of 3 eggs. Put the 2 cups of water in the double boiler. When it boils, add the corn starch mixed with 1½ cups of cold water. Cook ten minutes. Beat the yolks of the eggs and the sugar together, and add butter, the orange and lemon juice, and set away to cool. When cold spread between the cakes and frost with the whites of eggs. Rule For Frosting: To the white of 1 egg add 1 cup of powdered sugar. Beat until it will stick to the dish.—Mrs. A. V. Gude, Atlanta.

Washington Fritters.—Two cups milk, 2 cups flour, 3 tablespoons sugar, 4 eggs well beaten, a little salt, ½ teaspoon of cinnamon. Beat the sugar into the yolks. Add milk, salt and seasoning; the flour and whites alternately. Beat hard for three minutes. Have ready plenty of lard in a deep vessel, make very hot. Make the batter into small balls and drop into the fat and cook quickly. Serve on a napkin with pulverized sugar sprinkled over them.—Mrs. Junius Oglesby, Atlanta.

Strawberry Sponge.—Dissolve a small quantity of gelatine in as little water as possible. Dip as many ripe strawberries in it as will line a two-quart mold. Take 6 ounces of fine sugar and 1 quart of strawberries rubbed together till smooth, 1 pint of whipped cream and 2 ounces of gelatine dissolved and mixed with the cream. Beat these all together and pour into the mold, previously lined with the berries. Set on ice till ready for use. Turn it out on a dish and serve with whipped cream and angel cake.—Mrs. Walter B. Porter, Atlanta.

Puddings and Custards.

Swedish Timbales.—For the shells, use 1 cup of flour, ½ cup of milk, 2 eggs, ½ teaspoon of salt, ½ teaspoon of sugar, 2 tablespoons salad oil. Put all the ingredients together in a mixing bowl, and with a beater, beat to a smooth batter. Put the timbale iron in a kettle of hot fat for about twenty minutes. Take the bowl of batter in the left hand and hold it near the kettle of hot fat; with the right hand lift the iron from the fat, wipe it on soft paper, dip it into the batter, coating the iron to within ¾ of an inch from the top. Allow the batter to dry and then dip it in the hot fat, holding the iron a little sidewise until it is in the fat, then turn perpendicularly and cook until the batter is a delicate brown, or about one minute. Take the iron out the same way it is put in, being very careful not to drop the timbale into the fat, drain the grease off and lay it on paper to drain. Wipe the grease from the iron with a soft paper every time it is used. These may be filled with creamed oysters, creamed fish, green peas, macaroni, oranges, bananas, apricots, strawberries, etc., or mixed fruits with whipped cream over the top. They may be made at any time, and put in a dry, warm place, where they will keep indefinitely.—Miss Annie B. Northen, Atlanta.

Bananas en Surprise.—Select 6 firm, good-sized bananas, split them open carefully and remove the pulp. Beat the pulp to a cream, measure, and add half as many strawberries, 1 tablespoon of lemon juice, 3 tablespoons of powdered sugar, and 1 tablespoon of sherry or orange juice. Mix well together, being very careful not to make the pulp too liquid; then fill the banana skins and stand them on ice. To serve properly, the bananas should be tied with narrow ribbons of green and dull red. When strawberries are not in season, peaches, cherries or orange pulp may be used, changing the flavoring accordingly.—Mrs. Wm. M. Slaton, Atlanta.

Plum Pudding.—Half pound citron, 1 pound raisins, ½ pound butter, ¼ pound sugar, 3 eggs, 3 ounces flour, 3 ounces bread crumbs, 1 cup sweet milk poured over bread crumbs, spices to taste. Sauce: 2 cups granulated sugar, 1 cup fresh butter, ½ teacup of water. Put this on the stove and let come to boil. Beat the yolks of 2 eggs and stir to this and boil once. Flavor with wine or vanilla.—Mrs. James Judkins, Wetumka, Ala.

Exposition Pudding.—Mix well 12 eggs, wineglass of water with the yolks of 6 eggs, 1 tablespoon of butter, juice of 3 lemons, 1 cup of granulated sugar; boil together until thick, and when only milk-warm, pour into a deep dish lined with sliced sponge cake. After it is entirely cold, make a meringue of the 6 whites. Add a few drops of lemon juice to the meringue, spread on top the pudding and bake a delicate brown.—Mrs. George A. Parrott, Atlanta.

Strawberry Short Cake.—Make a good biscuit dough, rather short, into two layer cakes; bake a delicate brown. While hot butter them, slicing each cake in two, sweeten the strawberries, then mash them and spread thickly in the layers, reserving the largest to cover the top. Serve hot with plenty of rich cream.—Mrs. Livingston Mims, Atlanta.

Syrup Custard.—Five eggs well beaten, 1 cup of sugar, ½ cup butter, 2 tablespoons of corn starch or flour and 1 tablespoon of vanilla. Bake in rich crust. This quantity will make two custards.—Mrs. D. B. Freeman, Cartersville, Ga.

72   *Puddings and Custards.*

Steamed Apple Pudding.—Three juicy apples, 2 eggs, 1 teacup of sweet milk, 1 teaspoon of salt, 1 pint flour. Cut the apples in very small slices; make a batter about the consistency of waffle batter, using eggs with flour, yeast powder and salt. Put first in this dish a layer of batter, then one of apples. Continue this until the dish is full, having batter for the last layer. Steam for two hours and serve with sauce or sweetened cream. Flavor either one with nutmeg.—Mrs. Wm. B. Lowe, Atlanta.

Windsor Fig Pudding.—Five ounces of suet, 8 ounces of bread crumbs, 6 of sugar, ¾ pound of figs (dried), chopped very fine, 3 eggs, 1 cup of milk, ½ wineglass of brandy, 1 nutmeg, 2 teaspoons baking powder. Chop all very fine and stir thoroughly. Steam three hours in a tightly-closed steam pan.—Mrs. Wm. Hamlin, Detroit, Mich.

Gelatine Pudding.—One-half box gelatine, 5 eggs beaten separately, 4 tablespoons powdered sugar, 3 pints sweet milk. Dissolve gelatine in milk over the fire, then add sugar, then yolks, then add the well-beaten whites of eggs, just after the bucket comes out of the kettle of boiling water; then pouring into molds, set in a cold place until ready to serve. To be eaten cold with sweetened cream, flavored with sherry wine, or boiled custard flavored with vanilla. This will turn out of the mold, some clear jelly and some yellow. This is a very delicate dessert or a pretty dish for tea table.—Mrs. Tom Blanchard, Columbus, Ga.

Chocolate Pudding.—One quart milk, 1 cup sugar, ⅛ cup of Baker's chocolate, 1 whole egg and yolks of 3 more, 2 spoons of corn starch. Leave out a cup of milk to mix the ingredients. Boil these until the milk begins to thicken, then pour into your pudding dish. When cold, make a meringue of the whites, flavor with vanilla and pour over the pudding and set it in the stove for three minutes. A little chocolate beaten with the meringue is nice.—Miss Kate Clayton, Atlanta.

A New Dish.—Soak ½ pound French prunes in a very little water; put them on the stove with 1 tumbler of claret and a small piece of stick cinnamon. Simmer the fruit until tender, add 4 ounces of sugar. When it is dissolved, remove the stones and rub the prunes through a wire sieve. Take 2 ounces of bread crumbs, beat 3 eggs very light, and mix together. Add with the prunes. Put the mixture into a buttered mold, steam it about one hour. Turn into a dish, serving with whipped cream.—Mrs. Phil. Dodd, Atlanta.

Banbury Tarts.—Patty shells or timbales, one cup raisins chopped fine, 1 cup sugar, ¼ pound figs, ¼ pound citron chopped fine, juice of 1 orange, juice of 1 lemon. Add a little water and let the fruit boil until tender. When cool, add a little vanilla, 1 tablespoon sweet wine, fill the shells and put 1 large spoon of whipped cream on each one.—Mrs. C. H. Page, Atlanta.

Strawberry Sauce for Puddings.—One large tablespoon of butter, creamed. Add gradually 1½ cups powdered sugar and the beaten white of 1 egg. Beat till very light, and just before serving add 1 pint mashed strawberries.—Miss Bessie Draper, Atlanta.

Mince Meat.—One pound raisins, 1 pound currants, ¼ pound citron (sliced), 2 pounds lean beef boiled and chopped, ¼ pound each suet and leaf lard, 3 pints tart apples, sugar to taste, 1 heaping tablespoon of cinnamon, spice, mace, ginger and nutmeg, a little salt; moisten with sweet cider or sweet pickle vinegar. After cooking the beef, put all on the fire in a vessel and cook until the apples are well done, then it will not ferment.—Mrs. W. D. Smith, Oxford, Ala.

Creme Renverse.—One quart of milk, 6 eggs, 4 tablespoons of sugar, 1 teaspoon of vanilla, 1 teacup of sugar. Take the teacup of sugar and put in a small boiler with ½ pint of water; let this boil until it begins to burn or be a golden brown color; pour this into a mold, covering the sides of it with the caramel. Scald the milk, add the yolks of the eggs and 4 tablespoons of sugar and the vanilla. Pour into the mold and set it in a pan of water and bake in a hot oven. When cold turn it out on a dish. P. S.: 1½ pints of milk and 4 eggs make a good-sized pudding.—Mrs. H. H. Tucker, Atlanta.

Windsor Pudding.—Take of apples, currants, suet, raisins and a cold Swiss or French roll, each ½ pound, peel and juice of 1 lemon, 1 glass of sherry wine, ½ teaspoon of nutmeg, and pinch of salt. Grate the roll and add to the suet finely chopped, the nutmeg and lemon juice. Stone and mince the raisins, apply very fine. Add these, then the currants, wine and eggs well beaten. Mix thoroughly and boil in a pudding dish. Sift white sugar over the pudding.—Mrs. O. H. Lochrane, Atlanta.

Nesselrode Pudding.—Forty chestnuts, 1 pound of sugar, flavoring of vanilla, 1 pint of cream, yolks of 12 eggs, 1 glass of maraschino, 1 ounce candied citron, 2 ounces of currants, 2 ounces of stoned raisins. Blanch the chestnuts in boiling water, remove the nuts and pound until smooth, adding a few spoonfuls of the syrup; then rub through a fine sieve and mix them in a basin with a pint of syrup, made from 1 pound of sugar flavored with vanilla, 1 pint of cream and the yolks of 12 eggs. Set this mixture over a slow fire, stirring it without ceasing until the eggs begin to thicken (without allowing them to curdle), then take it off. When it is cold, put it into the freezer, adding the maraschino and make the mixture set, then add the sliced citron, currants and raisins to whole. Then add a plate of whipped cream mixed to the whites of 3 eggs, beaten to a froth. When the pudding is perfectly frozen, put into a mold, pack so it will become hard, and serve.—Mrs. Henry W. Grady, Atlanta.

Delightful Sauce.—One-half cup of butter, ½ cup of sugar. Beat them together. Add the yolks of 2 eggs well beaten. Pour on a cup of boiling wine, or if you have no wine, put ¾ cup of whisky, or you may instead use either a teaspoon of lemon or vanilla.—Mrs. Mary P. Cooper, Washington, Ga.

Ginger Pudding.—One cup of molasses, 2 cups of brown sugar, 1½ cups sweet milk, 1 cup butter and lard mixed, 6 cups sifted flour, 1 level teaspoon of soda, 2 teaspoons of ginger, 2 teaspoons of baking powder, 3 eggs.—Miss Daisy Merrill, Atlanta.

Jeff Davis Pudding.—Two cups of flour, 1 cup of raisins, 1 cup of currants, 1 cup of molasses, 1 cup suet, 1 cup sweet milk, 1 small teaspoon of soda. Put soda in molasses, then add flour alternately with milk, suet next, fruit last; put in thin cotton bags or molds, and steam for two hours.— Miss Carrie M. Merrill, Atlanta.

Puddings and Custards.

Plum Pudding—Two cups flour, 1 heaping cup of bread crumbs, 1 cup of molasses, 1½ cups stoned raisins, ½ cup citron (cut fine), 1 cup suet chopped fine, 1 cup sweet milk, 1 tablespoon soda, 1 teaspoon salt, 1½ teaspoons of cloves and cinnamon; steam two and a half hours. To be eaten with butter sauce.—Mrs. J. H. Porter, Atlanta.

Plum Pudding.—This pudding is best when prepared, all but eggs, the day before using. Three-fourths pound picked and finely-chopped suet, ¾ pound of stoned raisins, ¾ pound of currants, ¼ pound of citron cut in small slices, ¾ pound of powdered sugar, ¾ pound of bread crumbs grated, 1 lemon, grated yellow rind and juice, 1 tablespoon of powdered mace and cinnamon mixed and 2 powdered nutmegs, 12 eggs beaten separately. Steep allspice in ½ pint of mixed wine and brandy over night closely covered. Beat wine and eggs together until thick and smooth, then add bread crumbs. Mix with the sugar, grated yellow rind and juice of lemon, then add gradually prepared ingredients, stirring hard. Butter pudding mold, fill with mixture and boil four hours. Sprinkle hot dish with powdered sugar. Turn out pudding; pour ½ pint warm rum and light when taking to the table. This is sufficient for twenty persons.—Mrs. Willie Conyers Cook, Inman Park.

Jeff Davis Pudding.—Put 1 pint milk on fire and when it boils, stir in 2 tablespoons of flour wet in a little cold milk. Let thicken. Take from the fire and stir in ½ pound of sugar, ¼ pound of butter and 6 eggs well beaten. The whites beat to a stiff froth and add just before baking. Flavor with vanilla. Serve with wine sauce.—Miss Lucy Cook Peel, Atlanta.

MRS. CHARLES A. COLLIER,
Member of Woman's Board.

Trifle.—Make a boiled custard of corn starch, almost as thick as blanc mange. When thoroughly cold, flavor to taste. Have ready a sponge cake, syllabub and 1 pound of almonds blanched and shaved in thin slices with a knife. Cover the bottom of a glass dish with custard, cover the custard with thin slices of cake, the cake with syllabub and so on, custard, cake and syllabub in alternation, sprinkling almonds between each layer until the dish is filled, syllabub on top. It is better when prepared several hours before it is used and best when made over night and kept in a very cool place.—Mrs. Earnest Woodruff, Inman Park.

Prune Souffle.—Thirty-five prunes, 1 cup granulated sugar, 2 teaspoons of corn starch, whites of 9 eggs. After washing prunes thoroughly, put in soak over night and then cook them in same water until soft. Stone and mash. Add sugar, corn starch, the whites of eggs beaten to a stiff froth. Boil for three-fourths of an hour. Serve cold with whipped cream.—Mrs. J. Carroll Payne, Atlanta.

Strawberry Tapioca.—To 1 cup of granulated tapioca add 2 cups of cold water; soak a half hour. Put into a porcelain kettle and add 3 cups of milk warm water. Let cook till clear as jelly. Add a pinch of salt and 1 heaping cup of sugar. Cook a few minutes and pour into a vessel and let cool. When cold add 1 quart of strawberries mashed and sweetened to taste, and the juice of 1 lemon. Mix well with the tapioca and put on ice. Whip 1 pint of rich cream, flavor with vanilla or sherry. Serve with the strawberry tapioca. It can be made with any fruit.—Mrs. Samuel Stocking, Atlanta.

Swiss Pudding.—One teacup of flour, 4 tablespoons of butter, 3 of sugar, 1 pint of milk, 5 eggs, the rind of a lemon; grate the rind of the lemon into the milk, which put in the double boiler; rub the flour and butter together, pour the boiling milk on this, and return to the boiler; cook 5 minutes, stirring the first 2; beat the yolks of the eggs and sugar together, and stir into the boiling mixture; remove from the fire immediately; when cold, add the whites of eggs beaten to a stiff froth, and pour into a 3-quart mold well buttered, and steam 40 minutes. Serve hot with cream sauce.—Mrs. R. D. Spalding, Atlanta.

GELATINES.

Charlotte Russe.—One quart rich cream, ¼ package Nelson's gelatine, whites of 4 eggs beaten to a stiff froth, sweeten to taste, add 1 wineglass of sherry wine and 1 teaspoon of vanilla. Soak the gelatine in ½ pint milk for twenty minutes and then warm till gelatine is dissolved. Line a mold with fresh lady fingers, whip the cream, eggs, wine, vanilla and sugar, and put it, cup at a time, into a bowl. When all is whipped, and the gelatine and milk is about milk-warm, stir the latter into the former lightly and fill the mold.—Miss Hattie Root.

Spanish Cream.—One-fourth box Hazard's gelatine, soak in 1 cup of water, 1 quart milk, 3 eggs, 6 tablespoons of sugar, 1½ teaspoons of vanilla. Put milk on to boil in double boiler, separate eggs. In yolks, put 3 tablespoons of sugar and vanilla, stir well. In whites, beat 3 tablespoons of sugar until stiff. When milk boils, put in gelatine, then yolks, then whites. Stir until stiff. Put in mold. Serve with cream.—Mrs. Chas. Runnette, Inman Park.

Wine Jelly.—Half ounce red gelatine, ½ ounce white gelatine mixed, the juice of 1 lemon. Pour ½ pint of cold water over this and let it stand half an hour. Pour over it 1 pint boiling water, ½ pound sugar, ½ pint sherry wine. Strain through a bag into a mold. Set it away to get cold.—Mrs. J. F. Burke, Atlanta.

Noszky Cream.—Twelve eggs, 3¼ pounds of granulated sugar, 2 lemons, 2 ounces of gelatine, red or white, ½ pint of sherry wine. Separate the eggs, the yolks beaten with the sugar for a half hour. Grate the lemon peeling and strain the juice together. Dissolve the gelatine in the wine, warming it a little. Beat the whites of the eggs as stiff as possible and add to the yolks; gelatine added last. Pour in a melon mold and set in a cool place. Serve with rich cream.—Mrs. Dr. E. L. Connally, West End.

Coffee Mousse.—One quart of whipped cream, 2 tablespoons of gelatine dissolved in 2 tablespoons of boiling water. Boil 3 tablespoons of coffee in a cup of milk, strain, mix with the gelatine. When cold add it to the whipped cream. Put in a mold, pack in ice and salt. The cream must be whipped solidly through.—Mrs. James Freeman, Atlanta.

Souffle de Russe.—One and one-fourth quarts milk, dissolve in it an ounce box of gelatine and cook until it is as thick as soft custard, having added the yolks of 4 eggs beaten light, with 4 tablespoons of sugar. When as thick as custard, add the whites of the 4 eggs beaten stiff. Take off the stove before adding whites. Stir very briskly and pour in molds to cool. Eaten cold with a sauce of whipped cream, flavored with wine.—Mrs. Houston Force, St. Louis, Mo.

Charlotte Polonaise.—Yolks of 3 eggs, 1½ pints of fresh milk, 3 heaping iron spoons of sugar, 1 tablespoon of corn starch, cook until it thickens, flavor with vanilla. Divide the above into two parts, stirring in 1 pound of blanched almonds chopped fine in one, and in the other 1 pound chopped citron, then spread between any white layer cake, alternate layers of citron and almond custard.—Mrs. Sarah P. Lea, Holly Springs, Miss.

Charlotte Russe.—One quart sweet cream, 1 coffee cup sugar, whites of 3 eggs beaten to stiff froth. Add to them sugar till about thickness of icing, putting remainder of sugar in cream, ¼ to ⅓ cup wine, ½ box gelatine dissolved in warm water until thickness of honey. Season with vanilla to taste. Add wine and vanilla to cream before beginning to churn it. After frothed cream and well-beaten eggs have been mixed together, add gelatine last, stirring gently until whole begins to stiffen; then pour into molds and set away in cool place.—Mrs. E. R. DuBose, Atlanta.

Ribbon Blanc Mange.—Dissolve ⅔ of a box of Knox's gelatine in a pint of hot milk, sweeten with ½ cup sugar. Now divide the milk into three parts. Into the first, put the whites of 2 eggs, previously beaten to a stiff froth, and flavor with lemon. Put the beaten yolks, flavored with vanilla, into another. Wet 3 good tablespoons of grated chocolate with a little warm water, flavor with vanilla, and add the remaining third of milk and gelatine. As each part stiffens, whip with egg-beater, turning into a wet mold; first whites, then yellows, then chocolate. Can color the white pink with fruit coloring, if you like. Serve with whipped cream.—Miss Carrie Williams, LaGrange, Ga.

Charlotte Russe.—If the weather is very cold, use ½ box of gelatine, soaked in a little cold water about half an hour. If moderately cold use ¾ box. Beat yolks of 4 eggs very light with 4 tablespoons of sugar. Beat the whites to a stiff froth. Churn 1 quart of sweet cream flavored with vanilla. Mix the whites with yolks, next the cream. Pour enough hot water on the gelatine to thoroughly dissolve it. When cool, but before it begins to congeal, pour slowly into the mixture. Stir constantly to prevent lumping, only a few minutes, however. Then pour into a bowl to congeal. —Mrs. John Durr, Jr., Montgomery, Ala.

Floating Island (English).—One-half pint of cream, 3 ounces of sugar, the juice and rind of 1 lemon grated, 2 French rolls, apricot jam, 4 eggs, damson jam, sherry wine. Beat the cream and sugar to a stiff froth; lay it at the bottom of a glass dish. Cut the rolls into thin slices, lay them on the cream, pour a little sherry over and spread with apricot jam. Put another layer of rolls soaked in sherry, and pile on this a whip made of whites of eggs and damson jam. Pile it as high as possible.—Mrs. Capt. John L. Clem, Fort McPherson, Ga.

Gelatine Jelly.—To 2 boxes of gelatine, add 4 quarts of water, 1 quart wine, 4 lemons, 2 quarts crushed sugar, 1½ ounces of stick cinnamon, 3 dozen cloves, 3 or 4 blades mace, whites of 6 eggs well beaten, also the shells. Stir constantly until the mixture boils, then do not disturb it until it boils thirty minutes, straining through flannel bag.—Mrs. Joe Hirsch, Atlanta.

White Charlotte.—One quart of cream, 1 pound of sugar, 1 ounce of gelatine, 1 wineglass of wine, 1 teaspoon of vanilla, whites of 6 eggs. Add a part of the sugar to the cream and whip to a stiff froth. Whip your eggs very stiff and add the rest of the sugar to them, and then whip them into your cream, beat well and flavor. Lastly, add the gelatine after it has been dissolved in the wine and half a cup of water. Beat all together well and set in a cool place to congeal.—Mrs. A. A. Dozier, Columbus, Ga.

Jellied Tangerines.—Peel 1 dozen tangerine oranges, very carefully removing as much as possible of the white skin. Divide into sections and remove the seed. Have ready a box of gelatine which has been soaked in cold water for two hours. Pour over it 3 teacups of boiling water, stir until thoroughly dissolved. Add 2 teacups of fine granulated sugar. When dissolved, add the juice of 1 lemon, 1 teacup syrup from canned pineapple (or syrup from fresh fruit). Strain mixture through double cheese cloth. Have ready as many tiny teacups as there are guests, and dip them in cold water; put two or three sections of orange in each and pour over enough jelly to cover well. Set in a cold place until serving time. Turn out upon pretty individual dishes, and garnish the base with whipped cream. Sprinkle a few crystallized cherries on cream.—Mrs. S. B. Hudson, Columbus, Miss.

Chocolate Cream.—(As made by Frau von Mach, Dresden.) One-half of a cake of chocolate grated, 1½ teacups of sugar, 1 quart of cream, 1 pint of milk, 1 tablespoon of corn starch or flour, 1 teaspoon of vanilla. Put the milk on to boil. Pour a little hot water over the chocolate and the sugar, stirring to a smooth paste. Then pour into the milk. Cook together until as thick as a boiled custard and stir in the corn starch, and when it boils up well once, it is done. Set away to cool, and when quite cold, stir into it the cream, which has been flavored previously with vanilla, sweetened to taste and well whipped. Do not stir much, leaving the chocolate in streaks showing through the white cream.—Mrs. Julius Brown, Atlanta.

Turkish Preserved Oranges.—One bitter orange to 3 sweet oranges. Weigh the oranges whole and allow sugar pound for pound. Peel the oranges neatly and cut the rind into narrow shreds. Boil in clear water until tender, changing the water twice. Squeeze the strained juice of all the oranges over the sugar. Boil enough to clarify the sugar; put in the rinds and boil twenty minutes.—Miss Emma Roberts, Atlanta.

Green Lemon Preserves.—Soak the lemons four days in salt water, then simmer them in pure water, do not let them boil. When tender, take out the pulp. Place them to drain while making a rich syrup. When the syrup is perfectly cold, pour over the lemons. Let it remain three days, by which time the syrup will become green. Drain the syrup off and boil over again; when perfectly cold pour over the lemons. This must be done three times.—Mrs. Abbie R. Hopkins, McIntosh Co., Ga.

Ogeechee Lime Preserves.—Cut off the extreme ends of the limes. Soak them three days in salt water, then three days in fresh water. Boil them till tender, add syrup, 1½ pounds sugar to 1 pound of limes. They require more boiling than almost any other fruit.—Mrs. Abbie R. Hopkins, McIntosh Co., Ga.

Small Orange Preserves.—Scrape the skin of the oranges with a knife so that the oil may escape. Soak them three days in strong salt water, then three days in fresh water. Boil in pure water till soft enough to take out the insides, which can be done with a teaspoon handle through a small opening in the stem end of the orange. Soak again in pure water one day and night. Then boil till very tender before adding the sugar; 1 pound of sugar to 1 pound of oranges. —Miss Lottie Hopkins, Atlanta.

Fruit Gelatine.—Prepare ½ box of gelatine for congealing. When nearly cold, pour over a bowl half-filled with pineapple, bananas, sliced orange and Malaga grapes, and allow to stand over night. Serve with a generous dash of wine.—Miss Gussie Wylie, Atlanta.

To Make Jelly Without Boiling.—One package Knox's gelatine, 1½ pounds of granulated sugar, 1 pint sherry wine, 3 lemons, 1 pint of cold water and 1 quart boiling water. Put the gelatine in a bowl with the juice of the lemon and the rind pared thin and the sugar. Pour over this 1 pint cold water. Let it stand an hour or two. Then pour on the boiling water and stir until the jelly is dissolved, then add the wine and set aside to congeal.—Mrs. Clarendon Gould, Baltimore.

Charlotte Russe.—One-fourth of a tumbler of Nelson's gelatine; cover this with morning's milk and leave to dissolve; 1 pint of cream, whites of 5 eggs. Whip the cream after it has been sweetened and flavored with sherry or

MRS. DANIEL NORWOOD SPEER,
Member Committee on Agriculture and Horticulture.

vanilla. Have the eggs beaten to a stiff froth, gradually adding cream to the whites until all has been used. Then strain into this the gelatine and milk. A coffee strainer is best to use. Stir this in thoroughly. Set the gelatine on the back of the stove to thoroughly melt while the other work goes on. It should be cooled before using, until not warmer than new milk.—Mrs. Margaret Newman, Atlanta.

Pineapple Charlotte.—One quart of whipped cream, ¾ of a box of gelatine in 1 pint of sweet milk, 1½ cups of sugar, beaten with yolks of 6 eggs. Beat the whites of eggs very light. Stir all together and place on stove, letting it come to the boiling point. Then remove and place on ice. As it begins to congeal, add the whipped cream and 1 can of grated pineapple, draining off the syrup. A little grated cocoanut is an addition. Flavor with a little wine or vanilla.—Mrs. M. G. Kent, Selma, Ala.

Velvet Cream.—Dissolve 1 package of gelatine in cold water. Add 1 quart boiling water, juice of 8 lemons and 2 cups of pulverized or granulated sugar. Put on stove ½ gallon of fresh sweet milk and when just to a boil take off and add the white of 1 egg, beaten to a stiff froth and sweeten to taste. Put this compound of milk, etc., in freezer. Add gelatine solution and finish freezing process.— Mrs. J. T. Clark, LaGrange, Ga.

CHAFING DISH RECIPES.

How to Use a Chafing Dish.—When the dish is placed on the table, either before the host or hostess as the occasion may demand, have all the necessary materials. Butter may be made into balls, each ball representing 1 ounce. These arrange in a pretty dish on the right. If cream is to be used, measure and put in a little pitcher on the left. Bottles containing sauces and catsups or wine, should also be placed on the left, as well as large materials, such as lobsters and cheese. This saves much time and confusion. See that the lamp is filled and matches are at hand before being seated. When recipe calls for butter and flour, rub them together and put in a dish before serving them. If butter is to be browned, put it in dish first, then have the flour in a pretty bowl to be added later. Use for stirring a long-handled, polished wooden spoon. This will enable you to work easily and quietly. If you use a light metal dish, it becomes necessary at times to use the hot water pan; but with a heavy silver dish, this is unnecessary.—Mrs. Frederick F. Lyden, Baltimore, Md.

Quick Curry of Oysters.—Drain 25 fat oysters, put them in a bowl on a saucer at left, have a clove of garlic and a tablespoon of chopped pepper. Put into the dish 2 tablespoons of butter. When hot, not brown, add oysters. Sprinkle over 1 teaspoon curry, pepper and salt. Rub the spoon with the garlic and stir until boiling. Serve from dish.—Mrs. Frederick F. Lyden, Baltimore, Md.

Welsh Rarebit.—Two tablespoons of butter, 2 of flour, ½ pound of grated cheese, ½ teaspoon of salt, ¼ of red pepper, ¼ of mustard, 1 cup of cream, ⅔ teacup of ale or beer. Melt the butter in your chafing dish, add the flour gradually, then the cream and seasoning, stirring the cheese in last.—Miss Belle Newman, Atlanta.

Oysters Cooked at Table.—Use a chafing dish. Have the oysters carefully freed from all bits of shell. Put into the dish for a pint of oysters, 2 heaping tablespoons of butter, a dust of cayenne and the oysters. No salt is to be added unless the butter is very fresh. Stir the oysters until their edges begin to curl and then put out the lamp and serve them.—Mrs. John Bratton, Atlanta.

Oyster Stew.—In a chafing dish put 1 pint of milk, 1 tablespoon butter, salt, black pepper and a small piece red pepper. Let this stew and, while cooking, cut up small into it 1 bunch of celery. After this has stewed for about five minutes, put in 1 pint of oysters, dipping them up with a fork, so as not to get too much of the oyster liquor in the dish. Replace the cover and let them stew for about two minutes, then add 1 wineglass of sherry or Madeira wine and serve at once. Oysters must be opened raw.—Mrs. J. J. Bond, McIntosh Co., Ga.

Scrambled Eggs with Mushrooms.—Put 1 tablespoon of butter in chafing dish; when melted, add ½ can of mushrooms drained from their liquor and cut in pieces. Let them cook until thoroughly heated. Turn in 5 eggs beaten lightly without separating, and season with salt and pepper. As soon as they begin to foam, stir as for scrambled eggs until sufficiently cooked. Serve on buttered toast.— Mrs. Sarah Grant Jackson, Atlanta.

Anchovy Toast Eggs.—Beat 5 eggs slightly, add ½ teaspoon of salt, ½ teaspoon of pepper, and ½ cup of cream or milk. Put a heaping tablespoon of butter in the chafing dish, and when melted, add the mixture. Stir until the eggs are creamy. Spread slices of toast thickly with anchovy paste. Arrange on a platter and pour over them the scrambled eggs. If the crust is cut from the bread before toasting, and slices cut in squares, it has a daintier appearance.—Miss Sue Harwood, Marietta, Ga.

Deviled Tomatoes.—Cream 2 tablespoons of butter, add 1 level teaspoon of powdered sugar, 1 teaspoon of dry mustard, salt spoon of salt. Add ¼ of a salt spoon of white or cayenne pepper. Mash the yolk of 1 hard-boiled egg and add also 1 raw egg beaten slightly. Add slowly 1½ tablespoons of hot vinegar and cook until it thickens. Remove the skins from 3 tomatoes and cut in thick slices. Season with salt and pepper, dredge with flour and cook brown.—Mrs. Clifford Anderson, Atlanta.

Oyster Rarebit.—Clean and remove the muscle from ½ pint of oysters. Parboil them in a chafing dish in their own liquor until the edges curl and serve in a hot bowl. Put 1 tablespoon of butter, ½ pound of cheese (broken in bits), 1 salt spoon each of salt and mustard, and a few grains of cayenne into the chafing dish. While the cheese is melting, beat two eggs slightly and add them to the liquor. Mix this gradually with the melted cheese. Add the oysters and turn at once on the hot toast.—Miss Marion May, Atlanta.

Bellevue Stew.—One quart oysters, 1 cup oyster crackers crumbled, not mashed, 1 teacup sherry wine, 1 heaping saucer chopped celery, 1 tablespoon Worcester sauce, 1 generous tablespoon butter, pepper and salt to taste and a squeeze of lemon juice. Put oysters in chafing dish, cover and let them get hot, then add butter. After butter is melted, add other seasonings, putting in the wine just as it is ready to be served.—Miss Isa U. Glenn, Atlanta.

Welsh Rarebit.—One-fourth pound of rich cream cheese, ¼ cup cream or milk, 1 teaspoon of mustard, ½ teaspoon of salt, a few grains of cayenne, 1 egg, 1 teaspoon of butter, 4 slices of toast. Break the cheese in small pieces, or if hard, grate it. Put it with milk in a double boiler. Toast the bread and keep it hot. Mix the mustard, salt and pepper. Add the egg and beat well. When the cheese is melted, stir in the egg and butter, and cook two minutes, or until it thickens a little, but do not let it curdle. Pour it over the toast. May use ale instead of cream.—Miss Isabel Roach, Atlanta.

Chafing Dish Mushrooms.—Stir 1 large spoon of flour and another of butter in a stew pan together until thoroughly cooked. Open the can of mushrooms, and add ½ cup of the liquor with 1 cup of stock to the stew pan. Let it boil five minutes, seasoning with salt to taste and cayenne pepper. Then drain the mushrooms from the remainder of the liquor, empty into the stew pan, and cook until tender, about ten minutes. This makes an accompaniment to meat, or poured over toast.—Miss Laura Adair, Atlanta.

Stewed Oysters.—One quart oysters, 2 tablespoons butter, ½ pint cream, yolks of 2 eggs, teaspoon salt, pinch of cayenne pepper. Melt the butter in chafing dish over boiling water, stirring constantly. Beat together the yolks of the eggs and the cream, and add gradually, stirring all the time. As soon as it is thoroughly mixed, turn in the oysters and cook until plump.—Mrs. Julian Field, Atlanta.

Chicken Terrapin.—Put in the chafing dish the dark part of a turkey or chicken or goose, cut in small pieces, with ½ pint of cream or stock, and when it comes to a boil, stir in the following mixture: 2 tablespoons of butter, rubbed into a smooth paste with 1 tablespoon of flour and the yolks of 3 eggs and teaspoon of dry mustard, a little cayenne and salt mixed with a little cream or stock. Let simmer a few minutes (not boil) and then when ready to serve, stir in 1 wineglass of Madeira or sherry wine.—Mrs. Kate Grambling Hardin, Atlanta.

Bellevue Stew.—Three tablespoons of butter, 2 cups of celery, dried, 1 cup of cream, 2 tablespoons of cracker dust, salt, pepper to taste, 1 pint of oysters. Stew celery in butter until tender, add remaining ingredients, and serve as soon as oysters curl.—Mrs. Bertie Crew Inman, Atlanta.

Terrapin Stew.—Boil your terrapin tender, pick from it all the bones, and place the meat in a chafing dish. Add salt, allspice, pepper, mace and nutmeg to your taste. To five terrapins put 3 good tablespoons of butter, the yolks of ten hard-boiled eggs and work them together. When that has thickened, add 5 wineglasses cream. Boil the whole fifteen minutes, and then add 3 wineglasses of sherry or Madeira wine.—Mrs. A. C. Wylly, McIntosh Co., Ga.

FROZEN DESSERTS.

Maryland Ice Cream.—To each pint of milk, 2 eggs, 1 cup of sugar, 1 tablespoon of flour. Let come to a boil, then stir in the beaten eggs, sugar and flour. Let boil twenty minutes. When cold, put in 1 pint of cream after it is churned. Flavor to taste. I often vary this cream by the addition of ¼ pound of candied cherries.—Mrs. Annie Wilson Lyden, Baltimore, Md.

Frozen Desserts.

Fig Sherbet.—Three or four quarts of figs, mashed and sweetened, 1 quart lemonade. Freeze.—Mrs. S. E. Farley, Montgomery, Ala.

Vanilla Ice Cream.—One quart of cream, ¾ pound of granulated sugar, 1 quart milk, whites of 2 eggs, nearly 1 tablespoon vanilla. Beat the eggs light in a bowl, then add the cream, beat together, then add milk, sugar and vanilla, and freeze. The faster the freezer is turned at first or all through the process, the smoother the ice cream will be.— Mrs. E. R. L. Gould, Baltimore, Md.

Burnt Almond Cream.—Half gallon thick cream, 1 pint sherry, 1 pound of the thoroughly pulverized burnt almonds, sweeten to taste and freeze.—Miss Julia Collier, Atlanta.

Caramel Ice Cream.—Put 4 ounces of granulated sugar in an iron frying pan, and stir over the fire until the sugar melts, turns brown, boils and smokes. Have ready 1 pint of milk, turn the burnt sugar into this, stir over the fire one minute and stand away to cool. When cold, add ½ pound of sugar, 1 quart of cream and 1 tablespoon of vanilla. Mix well and freeze. When frozen, remove the dasher, stir into the cream 1 pint of whipped cream. Repack, cover and let stand for two hours to ripen. This will serve twelve persons.—Mrs. T. R. Mills, Griffin, Ga.

Macaroon Ice Cream.—One pint milk, 1 cup sugar, ½ cup flour, scant, 2 eggs, 1 quart cream, ½ dozen macaroons, 3 tablespoons of wine. Let the wine come to a boil, beat the flour, sugar and eggs together, and stir into the milk. Cook twenty minutes, stirring often. Set away to cool, after beating it in the air about ten minutes. Brown the macaroons in the oven, roll into crumbs; when cold, add with wine and cream to the thick mixture.—Mrs. John Millis, Washington, D. C.

Lemon Sherbet.—Half gallon cream, 1½ quarts cold water, ½ dozen lemons, 1½ pounds sugar; press juice from lemons, pour a little boiling water, let stand a few minutes, press out, let cool, mix and freeze.—Miss Sallie F. Hunnicutt, Atlanta.

Orange Souffle.—Put 2 cups of granulated sugar and 1 cup of water in a saucepan over the fire, stir until the sugar is dissolved. Then let it boil without stirring until the syrup spins a thread. Add 1 pint of orange juice and the juice of 1 lemon. Scald 1 cup of cream, add the beaten yolks of 2 eggs, stir them into the scalded cream. Take from the fire, cool and mix with the syrup. Stand away to cool and when thoroughly chilled, add the remaining cup of cream, whipped. Flavor with ½ a teaspoon of vanilla. Color delicately with yellow-colored paste. Turn into the freezer and freeze as a sherbet. Serve in glasses.—Miss Helen Louise Johnson, Philadelphia, in *Table Talk*.

Almond Bavarian Cream.—Custard: Four eggs, slightly beaten, 1 cup of sugar, 1 pint of milk. Soak gelatine (½ box) four hours if possible, drain water off and pour boiling custard on. Strain this and flavor with about 10 drops of bitter almond. Beat cream (1 quart) well, put over colander and drain. Place this cream in a pan over ice and sprinkle a cup of pulverized sugar and ¼ pound of grated almonds. Add custard gradually and fold in. Put in molds, and place on ice immediately.—Miss Mattie Smith, Griffin, Ga.

MRS. EDMUND L. TYLER,
Chairman Committee on Decorative and Applied Art.

Frozen Desserts.

Water Icing.—Three-fourths pound of pulverized sugar, juice of 1 lemon or orange and if too stiff, a few drops of water. This needs no cooking.—Miss Louise Speer, Atlanta.

Nesselrode Pudding.—One pound of large chestnuts, 1 pound of rich boiled chestnuts, 1 cup of sweet cream, 2 ounces of citron, 2 ounces of raisins, 2 ounces of stewed pineapple, ½ cup of maraschino, 1 teaspoon of vanilla extract, pinch of salt in the chestnut pulp. Slit shells of the chestnuts, boil them half an hour. Peel clean and pound the nuts to a pulp and rub through a sieve, moistening with cream. Then mix it with the boiled custard. Freeze this mixture, and when firm, whip the cup of cream and stir it in and freeze again. Then add the citron, cut in shreds, the stewed or candied pineapple, raisins, maraschino, and vanilla extract. Beat up and freeze again. Either serve in ice cream plates from the freezer or pack in a mold, and when well frozen, send to table in form. Turn out of mold in folded napkin on a dish.—Mrs. P. H. Snook, Atlanta.

Caramel Ice Cream.—Two cups of sugar, 2 eggs, 3 teaspoons of flour, 1 quart of milk, 1 pint of cream. Beat eggs, flour and 1 cup of sugar together until light. Put milk on fire; when hot, add eggs to it, and cook like custard. Take the other cup of sugar, put in a frying pan without water and caramel. When it is the color of syrup (a deep straw color), pour into custard. Whip the pint of cream. When custard is cold, mix cream with it and freeze.—Mrs. John W. Butt, Augusta, Ga.

Blackberry Water Ice.—(Delicious.) Let 2 quarts berries boil in ¾ quart of water until all flavor and juice is extracted from fruit. Strain, and when cold, make very sweet (or to taste), add juice of 1 lemon.—Miss Isabella Solomons, Savannah, Ga.

Strawberry Water Ice.—Mash 2 quarts berry pulp through sieve until seeds are left quite dry. Make thick syrup by boiling 1 pound sugar with ½ pint water until quite clear, adding when nearly cold to juice of berries. Lastly, add juice of 2 oranges or lemons. If this quantity of sugar does not make sufficiently sweet for general taste, more may be added before freezing.—Miss Rebecca Minis, Savannah, Ga.

Orange Sherbet.—One tablespoon gelatine, ½ cup cold water, ½ cup boiling water, 1 cup sugar, 1 cup cold water, juice of 6 oranges and 1 lemon. Soak gelatine in ½ cup of cold water, add the boiling water when dissolved. Add the sugar, the other cup of cold water and the fruit juice. When sugar is dissolved, strain and freeze. When it commences to freeze, stir into it the well-beaten whites of 2 eggs. A pretty addition is a little orange peel shaved very thin and cut in tiny pieces, added with the eggs. It looks well in the sherbet, when served.—Mrs. Louis Gholstin, Atlanta.

Apricot Ice.—One can of apricots, 1 lemon, ½ box gelatine, sugar to taste, 1 pint hot water. Take the stones out of the apricots and mash them through a colander. Pour the hot water over the gelatine, and when cold, mix with the fruit. Add the lemon juice and sweeten to taste. Freeze until the consistency of mush. Put in a mold and keep in salt and ice two hours before using.—Mrs. Edmund Tyler, Atlanta.

Frozen Desserts.

Edelweiss Cream.—Half pint milk, ½ cup flour, 1 cup sugar, 1 egg, 1 pint cream, ¼ cup sherry wine, ¼ cup seeded raisins, ½ cup preserved ginger, cut fine. When the milk has boiled, add cup sugar and the flour dissolved in a little cold milk. Let scald ten minutes, then add the eggs, well beaten. Boil two minutes longer. Let cool, then add ½ cup sugar, the cream and sherry. Beat all well with egg-whip. Freeze ten minutes, and add raisins and ginger. Then freeze as ice cream.—Mrs. John W. Grant, Atlanta.

Lemon Sherbet.—Two quarts milk, 5 lemons, 1 pound and a little over of sugar, whites of 6 eggs, pint rich cream. Boil milk, pour while hot over the sugar, grated peel of lemon, juice of lemon; add cream and whites of eggs, beaten to a stiff froth, when your milk has become very cold in the churn.—Mrs. T. J. Harwell, LaGrange, Ga.

Strawberry Ice Cream.—Use equal quantities of cream and strawberries. Run the berries through a sieve, then strain through a thin cloth. Sweeten to taste. Whip the cream, mix with strawberries and freeze.—Mrs. William Venable, Atlanta.

Strawberry Cream.—Take 1 quart of strawberries, crush, strain and set away until needed. Take 2 cups of sugar dissolved in as little water as needed; bring to a boil, and set off to cool. When quite cool, pour into a quart of good cream, flavored with vanilla. Whip or churn with syllabub churn until about a pint of stiff cream can be taken off and set away in refrigerator to drain. Into the remainder of the cream, pour the strawberry juice and freeze in an ice cream freezer. When well frozen, line a gallon mold for an inch in thickness with this frozen cream. Fill the center with the whipped cream. Cover the cream with a white paper, cut to fit, and press the cover to the mold tightly on, drawing a strip of buttered cloth 1 inch wide twice tightly around the mold where its top is fitted on. Pack the mold in salt and ice for several hours before needed, as it takes some time to freeze hard. Turn it out on a flat dish, garnish with strawberry leaves and clusters of the fresh fruit. This is a beautiful and elegant dessert. If strawberries are out of season, any other fruit may be substituted, or chocolate, as the cream may be colored with fruit coloring after the cream for the center is taken off.—Mrs. William J. Northen, Atlanta.

Fruit Delicacy.—Six well-flavored apples grated, 8 bananas grated, 1 can of grated pineapple, 1 dozen oranges, juice and pulp. Mix all together and sweeten to taste with pulverized sugar. Use juicy oranges. Prepare the orange cups in this way: Cut off a small piece from the top, and scoop out with a spoon all the juice and pulp. Mix this with other fruit. Strip out the white skin from inside of orange until you have a transparent cup. Now lay each cup in a glass saucer with a green lemon leaf or orange leaf under it. Fill each cup with the mixture and serve with a teaspoon.—Mrs. Harry Jackson, Atlanta.

Rennet Ice Cream.—Put 1 quart of sweet milk into a pan of boiling water until it gets lukewarm. Add 1 tablespoon of prepared rennet, 2 cups of sugar; beat well until it froths and is perfectly smooth. Season with lemon and vanilla. Add 1 quart of sweet cream well whipped. Whip all together with 1 egg. Whip until perfectly smooth, then freeze.—Mrs. Jake Burrus, Columbus, Ga.

Frozen Desserts.

Frozen Pudding.—Two cups of sugar, 2 eggs, 3 even table spoons of gelatine, 3 cups of milk, 1 quart cream, 4 tablespoons of wine, 1 pound of candied fruit. Soak the gelatine in enough water to cover until the water is absorbed. Put the milk on to boil, beat the eggs, flour and 1 cup sugar together, and stir into the boiling milk. Cook fifteen minutes, stirring often. Add the gelatine, cool; add the wine, 1 tablespoon of vanilla. Add 1 cup sugar to the cream. Beat well and strain into the freezer. When half-frozen, add the fruit cut in small pieces.—Mrs. Henry L. Wilson, Atlanta.

Peach Ice Cream.—Take soft ripe peaches; to each quart, after being mashed, add 1 pint of cream and 1 pint of rich milk with ½ ounce of gelatine dissolved and mixed in. Sweeten to taste, and freeze.—Miss Anne Speer, Atlanta.

Neapolitan Mousse.—Put a 3-quart mold in a wooden pail, first lining the bottom of pail with fine ice and a thin layer of coarse salt. Pack the space between mold and pail solidly with fine ice and coarse salt, using 2 quarts of salt, and ice enough to fill space. The ingredients are 1 quart of milk, ⅛ of a box of gelatine, 1 teacup of sugar, 4 tablespoons of sherry wine, ½ pound of candied cherries. Pour over the gelatine ⅓ of a cup of cold water, and let stand for two hours. Whip the cream first, putting in sugar and wine, then drain through a sieve, in order to insure no liquid being left in it. Now pour ⅛ of a cup of hot water over the gelatine which has been standing. When it is thoroughly dissolved, pour it in the whipped cream (first letting it cool) and stir until it begins to thicken, then pour a portion into the mold (after wiping it out). Sprinkle a layer of cherries cut in halves, then put in more cream and cherries alternately until all material is used. Cover the mold, pack with ice, throw a wet blanket over the pail, and let stand three hours. When served, dip mold into cold water, turn out on a flat dish.—Mrs. Dr. G. G. Roy, Atlanta.

Pineapple Ice.—Two small cans pineapple, 2 lemons, 3 cups sugar, half gallon boiling water, whites of 2 eggs well beaten. Mix thoroughly and freeze.—Mrs. Col. Garth, Columbus, Miss.

Raspberry Water Ice.—Boil 2 cups of water with 4 cups of sugar for 20 minutes. When taken from the fire, add the juice of 2 lemons and 3 cups of raspberry juice. As soon as cool, freeze.—Mrs. E. G. Thomas, Atlanta.

Strawberry Sherbet.—Mix with a pint of preserved or fresh strawberry juice, ½ cup of orange juice, ¼ cup of lemon juice, ¼ cup of sherry and the juice from a can of pineapple. Sweeten to taste and let stand for 2 hours if possible. Then mix with 1 quart of ice water and serve. Omit the sherry if desired. Fruit beverages are the most delightful drinks for hot weather, and are easily made, for they are but mixtures of different fruit juices, having the desired one predominate.—Mrs. W. P. Pattillo, Atlanta.

Ginger Sherbet.—Make a lemon water ice and freeze. Cut 4 ounces of preserved ginger into very small pieces, adding to it 2 tablespoons of the ginger syrup. Stir into the frozen ice, and pack.—Miss Irene Frazier, Inman Park.

Iced Cocoa.—To every pint of cocoa, made in the usual manner, add ½ cup of whipped cream. Beat it into the cocoa, sweeten to taste and let stand until cool. Serve in glasses partly filled with chipped ice.—Mrs. John Cowles, Athens, Ga.

Frozen Mint.—Make a plain lemon water ice, and when frozen very hard, add, stirring all the while, a mint julep made as follows: Bruise several tender sprigs of mint in 2 or 3 tablespoons of water sweetened with 1 lump of sugar; add 1 cup of brandy and 1 of sherry; let it stand 10 minutes and strain. When the julep has been added to the water ice, pack the freezer and allow the mint to stand some hours to ripen before serving.—Mrs. Jas. B. Conyers, Cartersville, Ga.

Frozen Cherries.—Take a quart can of cherries, using as red fruit as you can find, and mix with 1 pound of granulated sugar; stir until the sugar is thoroughly dissolved, add the juice from 1 can of pineapple, and 1 pint of water. Mix well; freeze as you do any frozen fruit.—Mrs. McDougald, Columbus, Ga.

Nougat Ice Cream.—Shell and blanch ½ cup of pistachio nuts and ¼ cup of almonds. Chop very, very fine with ½ cup of English walnuts. Make a rich vanilla cream, and when nearly frozen, beat in the nuts with a spoon, adding a few drops of pistachio extract.—Miss Caroline Holt, Washington, D. C.

Raspberry Water Ice.—Boil 2 cups of water with 4 cups of sugar for 20 minutes. When taken from the fire, add the juice of 2 lemons and 3 cups of raspberry juice. As soon as cool, freeze.—Mrs. Benjamin H. Hill, Sr., Atlanta.

Strawberry Ice.—Crush 1 quart of strawberries; add to them 1 cup of sugar. Let stand 1 hour. Boil 1 cup of sugar with 1 quart of water for 20 minutes; add to the strawberries, with the juice of 2 lemons and strain through a sieve. When cool, freeze.—Mrs. A. P. Thompson, Marysville, Tenn.

Orange Water Ice.—Boil 1 pound of sugar with 1 quart of water for 15 minutes; take from the fire, add 1 pint of orange juice and the juice of 3 lemons. When cool, strain and freeze.—Miss Nellie Wright, Atlanta.

Peach Water Ice.—Cut 8 good-sized, very ripe peaches in pieces. Mash them and add 1 cup of sugar; add the juice of 3 lemons mixed with ½ of a cup of sugar. Let stand 20 minutes. Add 1 quart of water, beat, strain and freeze.

CONFECTIONERY.

Creole Kisses.—Beat together 1 pound pulverized sugar, whites of 6 eggs (not beaten), 1 teaspoon of vanilla, for 15 minutes, and then add 1 teaspoon of cream tartar, and beat another 15 minutes, add one cup of chopped nuts (any kind), drop on paper (not buttered) and bake a light brown.—Miss Lillie Lochrane, Atlanta.

Chocolate Cream Squares.—Into a buttered tin that is 1 inch deep (square is best) pour a layer of chocolate and then 1 of the cream twice as thick as the chocolate and then 1 of the chocolate. Let each layer cool before adding the next. When all are hard cut into squares with a buttered knife. For Making the Chocolate: To 2 squares of Baker's chocolate chipped fine, add 2 tablespoons of granulated sugar and 1 of flour; melt together in an oatmeal cooker. When cooked so that it hardens on a cold plate it is ready for use. Flavor with a little vanilla. For the cream: 3 cups of

MRS. SALOUEL McKINLEY BUSSEY,
Secretary Committee on Agriculture and Horticulture.

Confectionery.

granulated sugar and 15 tablespoons milk. Boil over a quick fire, without burning, 5 minutes. When done stir until it is creamy. One-third this amount makes a nice icing for cake.—Miss Rebie Lowe, Atlanta.

Candied Figs.—Cook the figs in thin syrup until clear. Then put in colander and drain. Have ready a thick syrup made of best white confectioners' sugar. Take ½ dozen figs at time and dip in the syrup, laying on a wire strainer to drain of surplus syrup. Continue until all have been dipped a half dozen times, when all will be found to be nicely candied, quite equal in fact to anything from the confectioner. Peaches and grapes are also very nice.—Mrs. Virgie Moon, Hammond, La.

Sugared Pecans.—Two cups of pecans, 4 cups of sugar teaspoon of butter. Boil the sugar after dissolving; add the butter until it ropes, then remove from the fire and stir briskly until it becomes creamy, when the pecans are added. Pour upon a buttered dish; when cool cut into squares.—Mrs. M. A. Caldwell, Houston, Texas.

Nut Taffy.—One pint molasses, ½ pint sugar, ½ tablespoon butter. When done beat in ½ teaspoon soda and 1 quart of walnuts or hickory nuts.—Mrs. C. O. Tyner, Atlanta.

Chocolate Fudges.—One-fourth cake of Baker's chocolate, 2 cups of granulated sugar, 1 cup of cream or rich milk, butter size of an egg. Boil; stir constantly. Try it by dropping in cold water; if it hardens remove from the fire. Add 1 teaspoon of vanilla. Stir it hard for a few minutes and pour in buttered tins.—Mrs. F. M. Scott, Atlanta.

Confectionery.

Chocolate Caramels.—Two pounds sugar, butter ¼ pound, chocolate ½ cake, milk a large cup, vanilla a tablespoon. Let this stand on the back of the stove for half an hour, then put it on the front and boil hard for 10 minutes, stirring well; put in vanilla and boil 5 minutes longer. Have pan well buttered, pour in quickly. Mark off with bright knife.—Mrs. Frank Brochett, Washington, D. C.

Cream Candy.—Four cups sugar, 2 of water. 1 tablespoon of vinegar. Just before it is done add 1½ tablespoon of butter. Pull when nearly cold.—Mrs. Abner Camp, Grantville, Ga.

Caramel Candy.—Three cups of brown sugar, 1 cup of syrup, 1 cup of cream or milk and ½ cup of butter. When nearly done stir constantly. When done pour over marble and cut in blocks.—Miss Katie Stocking, Atlanta.

French Candy.—For 1 measure take 1 cup of granulated sugar and moisten well with cold water; into it stir ½ teaspoon of corn starch. Let it simmer till a spoonful will work with the fingers, when cooled in a saucer. Take off the fire and stir till cool; it is now ready for the nuts and fruit. Press the raisins open, make little balls of the fondant and put in; partly close the raisin and lay aside. Mash the nuts, make little rolls of the fondant and roll through the nuts. Open figs, make balls of the fondant, press into a shapely form and close the fig partly over it. Have grated cocoanut and make the fondant round; sprinkle with the cocoanut and slightly flatten. The fondant can be colored with chocolate and pink cake coloring, and flavored with anything desired. The more the fondant is stirred and worked, the nicer it is. Any one with deft fingers can make this candy and it is better than any that is sold.—Miss Nellie McLendon, Atlanta.

Peanut Brittle.—One pound granulated sugar, 1 quart peanuts, butter size walnut, pinch of soda, vanilla to taste. Put sugar in skillet with a little water to keep from burning. Let melt till it looks like molasses, put in soda and vanilla. Pour over peanuts, which are put in buttered pans. Thinner the better. Let cool.—Mrs. Lyden Meekins, Baltimore, Md.

Marshmallows.—Dissolve ½ pound white gum arabic in 1 pint of water, strain ½ pound fine sugar; place over fire, stirring constantly until syrup is dissolved, and of the consistency of honey. Add gradually the whites of 4 eggs, well beaten. Stir until mixture becomes thin and does not adhere to finger. Flavor to taste; pour into a tin dish with powdered starch, and when cool, cut into small squares.—Miss Aline Stocking, Atlanta.

Peppermint Drops.—One cup of sugar, crushed fine and just moistened with boiling water, then boiled 5 minutes; then take from the fire and add cream of tartar the size of a pea; mix well and add 4 or 5 drops of oil of peppermint. Beat briskly until the mixture whitens. Then drop quickly upon white paper. Have the cream of tartar and oil of peppermint measured while the sugar is boiling. If it sugars before it is all dropped, add a little water and boil a minute or two.—Miss Emily English, Atlanta.

Grilled Almonds.—Blanch a cup of almonds; dry them thoroughly. Boil a cup of sugar and ¼ cup of water till it "hairs." Then throw in the almonds; let them fry, as it were, in this syrup, stirring them occasionally. Will turn a yellow brown before the sugar changes color; do not wait an instant after this occurs or they will lose flavor; remove from the fire, and stir them until the syrup has turned back to sugar and clings to the nuts. (These are popular in France—used between courses alternating with salted almonds.)—Miss Mary Bert Howard, Atlanta.

Porceline Candy.—Two cups brown sugar, ¼ cup of water; let it boil enough to dissolve. Then add a teacup of milk and 1½ cups of hickory, or any other kind of nuts, and boil, stirring all the time. To tell when it is done, take out a little and stir; if it turns to sugar it is done enough. Pour in buttered pans and cut into squares just before it gets cold.—Miss Mary Frank Winship, Inman Park.

BEVERAGES.

Pineappleade.—Pare and slice some very ripe pineapples; then cut the slices into small pieces. Put them with all of their juice into a large pitcher and sprinkle among them plenty of powdered white sugar. Pour on boiling water, allowing a small half pint to each pineapple. Cover the pitcher and let it stand until quite cool, occasionally pressing down the pineapple with a spoon. Then set the pitcher for awhile in ice. Lastly strain the infusion into another vessel and transfer it to tumbler, putting into each glass some more sugar and a bit of ice. This beverage will be found delicious.—Mrs. Robert J. Lowry, Atlanta.

Royal Punch.—Two quarts black tea, 2 quarts claret, 1 quart sherry, 1 pint of California brandy, ½ pint of Santa Cruz rum, rind of 3 lemons, juice of 3 lemons. Sweeten and let stand 4 hours. When ready to drink, put in a can each of pineapple, strawberries, cherries and oranges. Add 3 quarts of champagne the last thing or 4 bottles of Rhine wine and 2 of Apollonaris water. These ingredients will make punch enough for 50 people. Another nice and much less expensive punch is as follows: To 1 bottle of Chateau Mægaux (Francois Cuzol & Fils Bordeau) add an after-dinner coffee cup of cherry cordial, superior quality, the juice and fine grating of 4 large lemons, about a pint of strawberries, and a cup of sugar, perhaps a little more. Fill the cups with shaved ice and pour the punch over it undiluted.—Mrs. Hattie Gould Jefferies, Augusta, Ga.

Roman Punch.—One quart weak tea, 1 pint sugar or more to taste, 1 pint claret, 2 tablespoons of rum, 1 pound glaced cherries, grated rind and juice of 3 lemons. Add the rum and cherries when the others are nearly half-frozen. Serve with whipped cream on top.—Mrs. Leonard Phinizy, Augusta, Ga.

Blackberry Cordial.—One gallon berries, 1½ quarts good spirits, 2½ pounds sugar, ½ ounce cloves, ½ ounce cinnamon. Let it stand 48 hours, then strain and bottle. Set it away 4 weeks, pour off and bottle again.—Mrs. J. W. Durr, Montgomery, Ala.

Blackberry Wine.—To each gallon of unbruised berries add 1 gallon of water. Allow them to stand 30 hours, remove whatever is on top; strain through a cloth; add 2½ pounds of good sugar to each gallon. Thoroughly dissolve and strain. Pour into vessels, allowing ⅛ vacuum for fermentation. Into 3-gallon jug put only 2 gallons. Close tightly and let stand until December, then open and pour off into bottles.—Mrs. A. A. Harman, Atlanta.

Fruit Punch.—The juice of 1 dozen lemons, 2 pineapples or 2 cans of same, 1 pint of strawberry syrup, 1 pint of orange flower syrup. Place all in the punch bowl with a large lump of ice, then pour in, after you have put in enough sugar to suit, 4 bottles of Apollonaris water. (This is a very delicious drink.)—Mrs. Cornelia C. Black, Deerland Park.

Brandy Peaches.—Take fine English peaches, scrub with a cloth dipped in cold water until all furze is removed, then prick to the stone in about a dozen places with a large needle. Drop in a kettle of cold water, put on the fire until water comes to a boil. *Be sure the peaches don't boil.* Take out with a perforated spoon, putting quickly between blankets, where they must strain for several hours. This will make them perfectly tender and yet firm. Then place in jars with layers of cut loaf sugar and pour over pure spirits or peach brandy. (Grandmother Barrett's Brandy Peaches.)—Mrs. Clark Howell, West End.

Raspberry Shrub.—One quart of apple vinegar, 3 quarts of berries; let stand 1 day, then strain. Then add to each pint 1 pound of sugar; skim it clear while boiling; let boil ½ hour. Put 1 wineglass brandy to each pint of shrub. When cold, bottle.—Miss Carrie Thompson, Washington, D. C.

Chocolate.—One quart of milk put on to boil; when it gets to boiling point add ¼ cake of chocolate; after it is melted (cut in small pieces and put in front of stove to dissolve), sweeten to taste. Boil all this for at least 30 minutes. Then add as you are ready to take up, yolk of 1 egg well beaten and 3 or 4 drops of vanilla. Stir constantly as you pour egg in; do not let it cook any more.—Mrs. T. R. Mills, Griffin, Ga.

Blackberry Wine.—To a peck of berries pour a quart of boiling water, let stand until cool. Strain through a coarse bag. Two and one-half pounds sugar to a gallon of juice. Put in a jug and let ferment until all black froth is thrown off. Keep a vessel to fill from; fill every day for 12 or 14 days. Pour off and add ½ pound sugar to a gallon of juice. Rinse jugs and put wine in again. Tie muslin cloth over the top, put in a cool place. Cork tight when done fermenting. Keep until old.—Mrs. Colin Frazier, Inman Park.

Noyean Cordial.—One pint alcohol, 1 pint water, 2 ounces bitter almonds pounded to a paste, 1 pound sugar, 1 pint of boiled milk, the peel of 1 lemon. Put in a pitcher, cover close. Stir every day for a week and then filter.—Mrs. Edgar Thompson, Washington, D. C.

Orange Cordial.—One quart alcohol, 1 quart water, the peel of 6 fresh oranges, removing as much of the inner rind as possible. Let it remain in a jug 3 months. Make a rich syrup and add to the contents of the jug after it has been strained. Bottle and cork.

Five O'clock Tea.—Select the best variety of tea, according to taste, Japanese Royal Garden being excellent. Boil your water quickly in a small kettle and pour over the leaves, allowing a teaspoon of tea to each cup. While the water is preparing, put a cube of sugar in each cup with a dessertspoon of fine old Medford rum and a slice of lemon. Let this mixture stand until the tea is drawn sufficiently strong. Then pour in the hot tea and you have a beverage that is delicious. In the event of any especial occasion, lemon juice may be used instead of the sliced lemon and the guest's initial cut out of the rind and allowed to float in the cup.—Mrs. Lollie Belle Wylie, Atlanta.

Persian Rose Leaf Punch.—One bottle of champagne, 14 blocks of loaf sugar, champagne glass of brandy, white wineglass of orange curacoa. Dissolve the sugar in a gill of boiling water, and when cool, add the brandy and curacoa. Partly fill the glasses with shaved ice, pour the champagne on the other liquors, stir well and fill the glasses at once. Add at once to each glass the leaves of 3 American Beauty roses. This is a most beautiful looking punch, and decidedly out of the ordinary. A frozen Turkish rose leaf punch is not so good to look upon, but, if anything, a nicer punch to serve.—*Table Talk.*

Turkish Punch.—To the ordinary Roman punch, when frozen, add 1 can of preserved Turkish rose leaves. Stir them in with a spoon, and if the punch then seems too sweet, add lemon juice. The cans of rose leaves are small, but the flavor is very strong, and 1 can will be sufficient for the quantity of punch for 16 people.—Mrs. Clarendon Gould, Baltimore, Md.

Regent's Punch.—One pound of loaf sugar, or rock candy, 1 large cup of strong black tea (made), 3 wineglasses of brandy, 3 wineglasses of rum, 1 bottle champagne, juice of 2 oranges, juice of 3 lemons, a large lump of ice.—Mrs. Capt. John L. Clem, Fort McPherson, Ga.

Beverages.

Raspberry Vinegar.—Soak 3 quarts red raspberries in 1 quart vinegar for 24 hours. Strain and add 3 more quarts berries. Let this stand 24 hours—then strain. Put in 1 cup sugar to every cup juice and boil twenty minutes.— Mrs. Richard Peters, Atlanta.

Chocolate.—Six tablespoons of grated chocolate, 1 pint boiling water, 1 pint boiling milk, ½ cup sugar, a pinch of salt, a dessertspoon of corn starch. Put sugar, salt and dry chocolate together, dissolve gradually in little hot water; add milk and let it boil together 1 minute. Dissolve corn starch in 2 tablespoons of milk reserved from the pint; add to the boiling mixture and stir constantly until it all boils up. Serve with whipped cream.—Mrs. Charles Price, Salisbury, N. C.

Spanish Cream.—Soak ¼ box Knox's gelatine in cold water (cover it well) 15 minutes; heat 1 pint of milk, and strain gelatine into it the first thing; then beat the yolks of 2 eggs with 2 tablespoons sugar, and cook like boiled custard; as soon as cooked, pour immediately into a pitcher, then add whites of eggs and flour. Pour into molds; serve with whipped cream.—Mrs. Arthur M. Tinker, North Adams, Mass.

Ratifia.—Take 1 gallon of best brandy, 1 quart of Madeira wine, 1 quart of Flontignac wine, 1 pint of orange flower water, 3 pounds of best loaf sugar, 1 pint of rose water, 2 peach kernels, blanched. Keep in the sun for 5 weeks, and bottle off.—Miss Mamie Boylston, Atlanta.

Imperial Punch.—One bottle of claret, 1 bottle of soda water, 4 tablespocns of sugar, ¼ teaspoon of grated nutmeg, 1 liqueur glass of maraschino, about 1 pound ice,

3 or 4 thin slices of cucumber with rind on. Put all the ingredients into a bowl or pitcher, and mix well.—Mrs. J. D. Stocker, Atlanta.

Balaklava Nectar.—(For a Party of Fifteen.) Thinly peel the rind of half a lemon, shred it fine, and put it in a punch bowl; add 2 tablespoons of sugar, and the juice of 2 lemons, the half of a small cucumber sliced thin, with the peel on; toss it up several times, then add 2 bottles of soda water, 2 of claret, 1 of champagne, stir well together with sufficient ice; serve.

Roman Punch.—Make a strong, sweet lemonade, using 1½ dozen lemons; add 1 pint of claret, 1 quart of champagne, ½ box gelatine dissolved in water, strain, add whites of 3 eggs; then freeze.—Mrs. Georgia Sykes, Aberdeen, Miss.

Corn Beer.—Boil 1 quart of corn until the grains crack, put the grains into a jug, and pour in 2 gallons of boiling water; do not use the water it was boiled in; add 1 quart of molasses, 1 handful of dried apples, 1 large spoonful of ginger; it will be ready for use in 2 or 3 days. If it is cool weather, set it in a warm place. You can use the same corn for several weeks; splendid with hot ginger cakes.—Mrs. D. S. Porter, Flowery Branch, Ga.

Tomato Wine.—Let the tomatoes be fully ripe; after washing well, let them stand 24 hours; then strain, and to every quart of juice, add 1 pound of good sugar; let it ferment again, skimming frequently; when clear, bottle. To use this, sweeten a glass of water to the taste, and add the tomato wine until sufficiently acid.—Mrs. E. C. Merrill, Atlanta.

Beverages.

Cherry Nectar.—To 4 pounds of the fruit, washed and picked (stone half the fruit), put 3 tumblers of white wine, or good apple vinegar; let it stand 4 days; strain through a cloth, and to a pint of juice, add a pound of loaf sugar; boil in a porcelain kettle a quarter of an hour; when cold, bottle and cork it; keep in a dry, cool place. To use, pour a tumbler half full of the nectar, add a few pieces of ice, fill with very cold water; a refreshing summer drink.—Mrs. Frank P. Rice, Atlanta.

Pineapple Beer.—Take the rind of a pineapple, put it into about 2 quarts of water; cover it, and set it aside for 24 hours; then sweeten to taste, bottle and cork; put it in the sun for 5 or 6 hours.—Miss Sallie Elkin, Lancaster, Ky.

Colonial Punch.—One quart of Madeira, 1 pint of brandy, 2 quarts of champagne, 3 sherry glasses of Jamaica rum, 1 pint of port; pour all the ingredients over 9 sliced oranges, except the champagne; sweeten, and set away in a covered vessel for 3 days; strain, add a large lump of ice to the punch bowl, and 15 minutes before serving, add the champagne.—Mrs. Edward Barnes, Atlanta.

Dripped Creole Coffee.—One tablespoon of ground coffee for each person to be served; place in the dripper of the coffeepot, and add to it 1 tablespoon of cold water; let stand one hour; have water boiling, and drip slowly; not more than 1 tablespoon of water should be used at any time; drip ¾ of a cup of coffee for each person, the other ¼ to be boiled milk, into which pour the coffee, and let boil 3 minutes; serve very hot. Proportions of brands of coffee: ⅔ Java, ⅓ Mocha.—Miss Daisy Hodgson, New Orleans.

MENUS.

BREAKFAST

Sliced Raw Tomatoes   Chicken Terrapin
Baked Potatoes Creamed
Asparagus Omelet
Pop-Overs   Coffee

Marinate the tomatoes and serve sliced on beds of watercress. Wash and drain the cress just before putting the tomatoes on it, that it may seem to have been just gathered; serve with French dressing. Prepare the eggs, etc., beforehand and make the chicken terrapin in the chafing dish on the table that it may be hot. Garnish with parsley and the whites of the eggs. Bake the potatoes; when done scoop out the inside, beat up at once with scalded cream and a little melted butter, heap on a plate, touch lightly with the beaten yolk of an egg, brown in a quick oven and serve with the terrapin. Instead of the asparagus omelet, can be served a sweet omelet, serving it as a course by itself.

Mrs. George Traylor, Atlanta.

BREAKFAST

Florida Oranges   California Grapes
Germea with Sugar and Cream
English Muffins   Light Rolls
Coffee   Tea
Spring Chicken Fried
Broiled Steak
Creamed Potatoes   Tomato Omelet
Waffles   Flannel Cakes   Syrup

Mrs. John L. Hopkins, Atlanta.

LUNCHEON

Roman Punch served in Ice Tumblers
Sweetbreads a la Creme
served in paper cases
Partridges on Toast   Salmon Croquettes
Sauce Hollandaise
Cheese Ramakin
Charlotte Russe
Black Coffee

Mrs. Clarendon Gould, Baltimore, Md.

LADIES' LUNCHEON

Bouillon
Oyster Coquille
Snowflake Crackers
Champagne   Ris de Veau Patties
Cream Sauce
Celery Salad   Ginger Ice
Quail on Toast   Saratoga Chips
Claret Wine
Chicken Salad   Beaten Biscuits
Olives
Salted Almonds
Jellied Tangerines with Whipped Cream
and Almond Cream Cakes
Cerise Menier   Pink Grapes
Coffee

Mrs. S. B. Hudson, Columbus, Miss.

LADIES' LUNCHEON

Strawberries, Sugar and Cream
Bouillon   Croutons
Vol au Vent of Asparagus
Persian Rose Leaf Punch
Compote of Chicken   French Peas
Potatoes en Surprise
Mock Crab Salad
Bananas en Surprise
Crackers   Coffee

Mrs. Joseph Thompson, Atlanta.

SUPPER

Bouillon
Fricasseed Oysters
Broiled Partridge   Ham Omelet
Potato Croquettes
Tomato Sauce
Celery Mayonnaise
Cracker Biscuit   French Rusks
Tea   Coffee   Chocolate
Neapolitan Ice Cream
Pink Angel Cake

Mrs. Porter King, Atlanta.

FAMILY DINNER

Clear Soup   Broiled Fish
Lemon Sauce
Scalloped Potatoes   Spanish Stew
Boiled Rice   Spiced Sweet Potatoes
Mayonnaise of Celery
Swiss Pudding   Creamy Sauce
Fruits   Coffee

Mrs. John L. Hopkins, Atlanta.

ANITA'S GAME COURSE

With Roast Partridges serve a sauce made as follows: Heaping tablespoon butter and same of sifted flour, rub well together; one half pint of broth, 2 teaspoons of each; mushrooms, catsup, cream and lemon juice. Put to boil, stirring well. Add beaten yolks of 2 eggs, stirring constantly and never allow it to boil after adding eggs. Cheese souffles are served with this, baked either in paper forms or stone dishes. Take 2 level tablespoons of butter, when melted stir in 1 heaping tablespoon of flour until frothy, but not brown, add one-half cup of milk gradually, 1 cup of grated cheese, one-half teaspoon of salt, cayenne, yolks of 3 eggs, beaten light. When about to serve, add the whites beaten stiff, and bake in a moderate oven 12 minutes.

Mrs. E. P. McIlheney, Houston, Texas.

LUNCHEON

Clam Bouillon
     Cheese Straws
Deviled Oysters   Sauterne
Sweetbread Timbales
French Peas
Imperial Punch
Broiled Chicken with Bernaise Sauce
Roman Potatoes
French Rolls (hot)
Tomato Salad with Mayonnaise
Rainbow Jelly with Whipped Cream
Almonds   Olives
Crystallized Ginger
Creme de Rose

Miss Corinne R. Stocker, Atlanta.

LUNCHEON

Raw Oysters
Soup
Baked Shad   Potatoes
Birds
Green Peas   Finger Rolls
Grilled Almonds
Apricot Ice
Asparagus on Toast
Brain Patties
Tomato Salad with Mayonnaise Dressing
Beaten Biscuit Croquettes
Olives
Ice Cream   Cake
Fruit
Cheese Straws and Coffee

Mrs. Charles F. Rice, Atlanta.

DINNER

Julienne Soup
Oysters a la Creme
Roast Lamb   Mint Sauce
Peas
New Potatoes   Lettuce
French Dressing
Strawberry Bavarian Cream
Crackers   Cheese
Black Coffee

Mrs. S. B. Hudson, Columbus, Miss.

GENTLEMEN'S DINNER

Blue Points on the Half-shell
Andalusian Soup
Broiled Pompano   Tartar Sauce
Roast Fillet of Beef with Mushrooms
Stuffed Tomatoes
Roman Punch
     Chicken Timbales
Cream Sauce
Lettuce with French Dressing
Royal Diplomatic Pudding
     Kentucky Chess Cake
Edam and Roquefort Cheese
Crackers   Coffee

Mrs. R. D. Spalding, Atlanta.

P. S.

Caramel Cake.—Whites of 8 eggs, 2 cups of powdered sugar, 1 cup of butter, 4 cups of flour (measure after sifting), 1 cup of sweet milk, 2 teaspoons cream tartar, 1 of soda; bake in 3 layers, good-sized pans. Filling: 3 cups C. sugar, 1 cup sweet cream, butter the size of a large egg, boil until thick. The above cake recipe can be used with the following fillings: 2 cups of sugar, water enough to dissolve, let boil until hard enough to pull like candy, try it in cold water, whites of 3 eggs beaten about half stiff; let the syrup stop boiling before pouring into the eggs, continue to beat until cold enough to spread. Very finely chopped raisins put in this is very nice, also nuts or figs; put the fruits or nuts in part of icing, saving part for outside, marsh mallow cut fine is also very nice put in icing between angel food.— Miss Carrie Merrill, Atlanta.

"Love Not" Palmer's Cake.*—Two and one-half cups of flour ⅔ cup of butter, 1 cup of milk, 1 cup of sugar, 2 teaspoons of baking powder, 2 eggs, ⅔ cake of chocolate (Baker's), 1 cup of sugar, ½ cup of milk; boil until thick, set away to cool, mix with batter, bake in layer cakes and stick together with chocolate or caramel filling.

Chocolate Filling.*—Boil ½ cup of sugar with 8 tablespoons of cream and ½ cake of chocolate grated, until it will stand; pour this over the beaten whites of 2 eggs, add 1 teaspoon of vanilla, beat until it thickens, put between layers over the top and sides.

Hinton's Caramel.*—Three cups of white sugar, 1 cup of sweet milk, 1 cup of fresh butter. Boil together until it

---
* "Inglehurst Recipes" from Mrs. F. D. Wimberly.

thickens, then remove from the fire, add 1 teaspoon of vanilla and whip until it is cold.

Cousin Ann Hill's White Cake.*—Whites of 14 eggs, 1 pound of sugar, ¾ pound of flour, ½ pound of butter. Cream flour and butter together, beat the whites and sugar together until it looks like icing, mix well and flavor with lemon.

Inglehurst White Fruit Cake.*—Whites of 8 eggs, 1 coffee cup of sweet milk, 2 coffee cups of sugar, 4 coffee cups of flour, 1 coffee cup of butter, 3 teaspoons of baking powder, 2 teaspoons of lemon extract, 2 grated cocoanuts, 2 grated nutmegs, 1 pound of citron, 1 pound of almonds, 1 glass of sherry wine. Add a cup more of sugar with the cocoanut. Candied orange peels and crystallized pineapple improves the flavor.

Wimberly Fruit Cake.*—Two pounds of flour, 2 pounds of brown sugar, 1 pound of butter, 3 pounds of raisins, 3 pounds of currants, 3 pounds of citrons, 14 eggs, 1 large cup of cream, 1½ tablespoons of cinnamon, 1½ tablespoons of spice, 1½ tablespoons of cloves, 1 tumbler of brandy, 1 tumbler of good wine, 2 grated nutmegs, 2 teaspoons of soda dissolved in a large cup nearly full of molasses. Chop raisins fine, rub fruit in flour and bake slowly.

Inglehurst Pound Cake.*—One pound of sugar, 1 pound of flour, 1 pound of butter, 1 pound of eggs, and one extra for shells; 1 teaspoon of cream tartar, ½ teaspoon of soda, 1 teaspoon of lemon; sift cream of tartar in flour; dissolve soda in a little water, and add last.

---

*"Inglehurst Recipes" from Mrs. F. D. Wimberly.

Inglehurst Dressing.*—One pint of vinegar, 1 tablespoon of butter, 1 teaspoon of mustard, 1 teaspoon of salt, 1 teaspoon of sugar, 1 teaspoon of black pepper, yolks of 4 eggs; rub the butter, mustard, salt, sugar and pepper together, beat the yolks with a tablespoon of water; when the vinegar boils, add the butter, etc., and stir in the yolks, and cook until the thickness of cream. Excellent for fish, vegetables, and ham.

Inglehurst Sally Lunn.*—One yeast cake dissolved in a tumbler of warm water, ¾ tumbler of warm milk, 1 tablespoon of butter or lard, 3 *heaping* tablespoons of sugar, 1 dessertspoon of salt, enough flour for a stiff batter, and let it stand in a warm place until well risen; keep beating it down until time to bake, put in a well-buttered pan, let rise, and bake in a quick oven.

Corn Pickle.*—Two dozen ears of tender corn, 1 head of white cabbage (small), 1 bottle of olive oil, 5 cents' worth of turmeric, ½ ounce of white mustard seed, ½ ounce of black mustard seed, ½ ounce of celery seed, 1 tablespoon of mustard; chop cabbage fine, cut corn off ears, sprinkle salt over layer of corn and cabbage, and let stand over night, then squeeze out of salt water, cover with vinegar, and cook until tender; when cool, squeeze out again; take enough vinegar and a pound of sugar, let come to a boil, and pour over the pickle; mix mustard seeds, mustard, turmeric, celery and oil with corn and cabbage, after squeezing the second time, and just before pouring on the boiling vinegar and sugar.

---

* "Inglehurst Recipes" from Mrs. F. D. Wimberly.

MRS. FREDERICK FOUNTAIN LYDEN,
Member Committee on Agriculture and Horticulture.

Stuffed Eggs.—Boil 10 eggs 20 minutes, peel off the shells and cut in halves to form two bateaux, remove all the hard-boiled yolks and put into a bowl; in an earthen saucepan, mix 2 well-beaten eggs, 1 tablespoon dry mustard, 3 tablespoons cream, 1 teaspoon salt, ½ teaspoon pepper (cayenne is best), 2 tablespoons olive oil, 2 of vinegar, one of sugar; boil until a thick custard, and mix with hard-boiled yolks; fill the whites with the mixture; serve cold.—Mrs. A. D. Adair, Atlanta.

Five O'clock Tea Sandwiches.—With a five o'clock cup of tea, one wants a thin, delicately flavored sandwich, and I have found this one entirely satisfactory and very popular. Cut your bread in thin slices and shape as fancy dictates after the crust is removed. Butter smoothly and lay on damp cloth until ready to fill. For a filling, use boiled ham, hard-boiled eggs and artichoke pickles in equal proportions. Cut the ham with a pair of sharp scissors into long, thin threads and slice the pickle in round, flat slices, cutting them very thin. Mix a dressing of mustard, salt, pepper, vinegar and celery seed and add a raw egg. Boil, and when a little thick add to the meat, pickle and eggs. Mix lightly and lay between 2 slices of bread. Tie with a ribbon.—Mrs. Lollie Belle Wylie, Atlanta.

Syrup.—One cup white sugar, 1 of good brown sugar, 1 of water. Mix well and let it boil 15 minutes, remove and flavor with vanilla.

Blackberry Pudding.—One-half pound butter, 1 pound brown sugar, 1½ pounds flour, 4 eggs, well beaten, 1 quart blackberries; cream the butter and sugar, add flour and eggs alternately, put in a baking dish, lay blackberries on top, bake in a moderate oven; in baking, the berries will be evenly distributed; serve with wine sauce.—Mrs. Henry Bryan, Dillon, Ga.

Crab Stew.—Pick a dozen crabs carefully, separate the fat from the other meat; rub the yolks of 2 hard-boiled eggs until mashed smooth, add to them a tablespoon of butter, and one of wheat flour, rubbing smoothly together; season with salt, pepper, nutmeg and a little onion; mix into this slowly 1 quart of milk, and set on the fire to boil; when it tastes cooked, put in the picked crabs, boil a short time, and just before dishing, add the fat.

Veal Cutlets.—Cut the cutlets an inch thick, and round them; beat the yolks of two eggs, dip the cutlets in the egg, take them out and strew over them grated bread, seasoned with salt, pepper, a little nutmeg, parsley, and thyme; fry brown; when the cutlets are taken out, stir a little butter into the gravy; serve hot. A little grated lemon peel is an improvement in the dressing.—Mrs. Henry Bryan, Dillon, Ga.

Tomato Beer.—Gather the tomatoes in the afternoon, wash and let stand until morning, then strain; put 2 pounds of sugar to the gallon of syrup; put in a vessel, and strain as fermentation rises to the top, until it gets clear, then bottle tightly; dilute with water when using, and sweeten to taste.—Mrs. M. A. J. Powell, Atlanta.

Cherry Bounce.—Fill demijohn with ripe cherries, unstoned, but without stems; cover entirely with white brandy, or fine whisky; cork, and let stand 2 weeks; pour off brandy or whisky in another vessel, then refill with brandy over cherries again; allow this to stand for 2 weeks, then pour off brandy or whisky, and mix with the other brandy or whisky; re-cover cherries with cold water, let stand 2 weeks; pour off and mix with first and second brandy or whisky; add 3 pounds of white granulated sugar to every gallon of juice, and stir until thoroughly dissolved; let stand for two months; rack off through strainer.—Miss Ella M. Powell, Atlanta.

White Cake.—Whip to a light cream 2 cups sugar and 1 nearly full of butter, add 1 cup sweet cream; sift flour twice, then measure out 3 cups of flour and 1 teaspoon of Royal baking powder; last, add the whites of 9 eggs well beaten, flavor with almond extract, bake in a moderate oven until cake leaves sides and stem of pan. A splendid white cake. —Mrs. Jennie E. Lumpkin, Central, S. C.

Julian Chess Cake.—Yolks of 28 eggs, 1 pound of butter, 1¼ pounds of sugar, 1 pound of dried currants, ½ pound of raisins, ¼ pound of citron, ½ pound mixed candied French fruit, ½ pound of figs, ½ pound of dates, 1 dessertspoon each of ground nutmeg, allspice, cloves and mace, 1 tablespoon of cinnamon, 2 tablespoons of rose water, 1 glass of wine. Make a rich puff paste, roll very thin and line jelly tins; fill with the above and bake in moderate warm oven. Each layer to be iced and put together with icing. Put spices in wine and let stand awhile.—Mrs. H. H. Kerr, Murfreesboro, Tenn.

Fruit Cake.—Twelve eggs, 2 cups of butter, 6 cups of sugar, 10 cups of flour, 2 cups of sweet milk, 2 teaspoons of soda and 4 teaspoons of cream tartar dissolved in the milk, 1 cup black molasses. Stir ½ teaspoon of soda into molasses, 4 pounds raisins, 2 pounds currants, 1 pound citron, 1½ pounds of dried figs, 1 cup blackberry jam, 4 tablespoons nutmeg, 6 tablespoons of cinnamon, 3 tablespoons of cloves, 3 tablespoons spice, 2 tumblers brandy poured over the spice before putting into the batter. Flavor to taste with vanilla and lemon. Bake slow. Just before it is cold, pour over 2 tumblers of some good wine to keep it moist.—Mrs. A. M. Robinson, Atlanta.

Tapioca Apples.—Prepare apples as for apple duck. Take 5 tablespoons of tapioca, let it soak 20 minutes in cold water. Put a quart of sweet milk on the fire, sweeten it a little, when near boiling, stir into it the tapioca with the well-beaten yolks of 6 eggs; beat the whites with 6 tablespoons of sugar to a stiff froth. When the milk has cooled a little, stir in part of the whites. Fill the apples with this and bake until the apples are done. In top of each apple pile a spoon of remainder of whites and return to the oven until a delicate brown.—Mrs. A. J. Orme, Atlanta.

Salmon for Dinner.—Take all the bones and skin from salmon; warm it without too much of the sauce that comes in can. Half pint of rich milk, into which stir two tablespoons of flour, 2 tablespoons of melted butter; stir all together, put on to boil and stir until thick. Chop up 2 or 3 hard-boiled eggs and put in dressing.—Mrs. J. M. Billups, Columbus, Ga.

Milk Yeast Bread.—Take 1 cup of meal, 1 cup of sweet milk; boil and stir in meal while hot; ½ cup of warm water stirred in, 1 cup of flour sifted in, then put that in a bowl and set in a warm place to rise. After it has risen, add 1 teaspoon of sugar, large spoon of lard and 3 pints of flour. Work as quickly as possible and be careful not to let the dough get cold. When it rises to the top of pan, bake in a moderate oven.—Miss Lena P. Johnson, Inman Park.

Corn Meal Muffins.—One and one-half pints of buttermilk, stir in 1 teaspoon of soda until it foams. Have ready 2 eggs well beaten and pour in enough salt to taste. Add enough corn meal to make a nice batter. Melt piece of lard size of small hen egg and pour in batter boiling hot.—Miss Sallie Elkin, Lancaster, Ky.

Corn Loaf.—Three cups meal, 1 cup flour, 1 cup dark syrup, 2 teaspoons yeast powder, 1½ cups milk, salt. Put in a covered bucket, place bucket in a kettle of water, boil steadily for 2½ hours.—Mrs. Paul Romare, Atlanta.

Kiss Pudding.—One quart sweet milk boiled in custard kettle, stir into it 4 tablespoons corn starch dissolved in a little cold water or milk. Add the well-beaten and strained yolks of 4 eggs. Beat the whites to a stiff froth with 1 teacup of pulverized sugar and 1 teaspoon of vanilla. Spread on top of pudding. Set in quick oven and brown. Sprinkle with grated cocoanut and set aside to cool. Serve after 3 or 4 hours.—Mrs. G. A. Cabaniss, Atlanta.

A Swedish Dessert.—Two tumblers of acid fruit jelly, 1 quart boiling water, and a little sugar, if too acid. When thoroughly melted, pour in 4 or 5 tablespoons corn starch mixed in water, boil till it thickens, pour into dish or molds and serve with whipped cream.—Miss Marie Romare, Atlanta.

Restorative Jelly.—One-half box gelatine, 1 cup port wine, 1 tablespoon of powdered gum arabic, 2 tablespoons of lemon juice, 3 tablespoons of sugar, 2 cloves. Put all together in a glass jar, and cover closely. Place the jar on a trivet in a kettle of cold water. Heat it slowly and when the mixture is dissolved, stir well and strain. Pour into a shallow dish, and when cool cut it into small squares. This is good for an old person or a very weak patient.—Mrs. Dr. Robert Ridley, Atlanta.

Charlotte Russe.—Soak 1 ounce of gelatine in a pint of sweet milk for 1 hour, place the same over the fire and keep stirring until the gelatine is thoroughly dissolved, then remove, and when nearly cold beat thoroughly with an egg-beater. Flavor 1 quart of cream with 1 heaping teaspoon of extract vanilla, wine and pulverized sugar to taste. Pour the 2 mixtures together and whip thoroughly, then into molds lined with sponge cake.—Mrs. R. S. Rust, Atlanta.

Swiss Biscuit.—Dissolve half a yeast cake in a half teacup of warm water; beat the yolks of 2 eggs very light, and add to the yeast, with the sugar, salt, and 1 tablespoon of butter, and enough flour to make a soft dough; let it rise, as for rolls; beat the whites stiff, and add to the risen dough with more flour; roll out like biscuit, spread butter over it, and fold over; cut with biscuit cutter, put in buttered pans, and when light, bake them a light brown.—Mrs. Wm. G. Elkin, Aberdeen, Miss.

Corn Wafers.—To 1 cup of corn meal add 1 tablespoon of flour, a little salt, and sufficient sweet milk to make a soft

dough; bake in wafer irons a light brown on both sides.—
Mrs. P. Brown, Gainesville, Ga.

Swiss Splits.—Two medium-sized Irish potatoes; boil in 1 pint or 1½ pints of water until soft; pass through a vegetable strainer into a bowl; add to it a teacup of the potato water, scalding hot; 1 tablespoon of sugar, 1 teaspoon of salt, ¾ cup of yeast; mix well, and add 1 pint of flour; if too stiff to work with spoon, add little more potato water; make up about 9 o'clock A. M., and set to rise until 1 o'clock P. M.; when well risen, break into dough 3 eggs; mix well, and add 1 good tablespoon of lard and 2 pints of flour; work until all are well mixed, then set again to rise; at 5 P. M., work again, adding a little flour, if needed, and make dough the ordinary consistency of light bread; roll out as for biscuit, butter the upper side, and cut out your rolls with a biscuit cutter, and place 2 together (buttered sides touching); set to rise again, and when risen bake for supper.—Mrs. Sue B. Hudson, Columbus, Miss.

Some Simple Remedies From a Texas Lady.—For Indigestion: One-quarter of a teaspoon of soda, 10 drops of peppermint in ⅓ of a glass of water. For Sick Headache: The juice of 1 lemon in a half glass of water, either hot or cold; a little sugar and ¼ of a teaspoon of soda.

Cold Cream.—Three ounces almond oil, 3 ounces of rose water, 3 ounces of mutton suet, ½ ounce of white wax, ½ ounce of spermaceti; perfume with any extract preferred; put all together in a saucepan and heat until melted; don't let boil; then beat until a white, smooth cream.—Mrs. Dr. J. B. S. Holmes, Atlanta.

Baking Powder.—Nine ounces cream tartar, 4 ounces of soda, 6 ounces of flour; sift six times.—Mrs. Charles Runnette, Inman Park.

Gruel or Beef Tea.—Take 2 tablespoons of oatmeal, with 3 of cold water, and mix them thoroughly; then add 1 pint of strong boiling beef tea or milk; boil 5 minutes, stirring well to prevent the oatmeal from burning; then strain.—Dr. J. J. Linscott, Holton, Kansas.

Pear Butter.—To 7 pounds of pears, peeled and quartered, put ½ pint cider vinegar, 1 ounce allspice, 1 ounce cloves, 1 ounce stock cinnamon, ¼ ounce mace; tie the spices in a piece of muslin, and let them boil with the pears and vinegar, until the pears can be mashed to a pulp; take out the spice, and add 3 pounds of sugar, and boil to a marmalade.—Mrs. J. L. Hopkins, McIntosh Co., Ga.

Coffee.—Two-thirds Java, and ⅓ Mocha, whites and shells of 2 eggs to 3 pounds; mix, and then leave in pan to dry; put coffee in pot and pour a little cold water over it; then pour in the boiling water, not to the brim.—Mrs. Elizabeth Collins, Baltimore, Md.

Breakfast Dish.—Take equal quantities of apples and onions, stew apples and fry onions in lard till brown; then add the apples to the onions, and continue stewing and mashing till all are well cooked; serve hot. Nice side dish for breakfast.—Mrs. T. S. Quarterman, McIntosh Co., Ga.

Mock Olives.—Gather plums just before ripening; soak them over night in weak brine, drain and pour over them, boiling hot, this pickle: to every quart vinegar, 2 tablespoons white mustard seed, ½ teaspoon whole cloves, tied in a cloth. Simmer for 15 minutes, let them remain in brine 24 hours; reheat and return to plums; put up in small jars. They mould after being opened.—Mrs. T. S. Quarterman, McIntosh Co., Ga.

A Pretty Tea Dish.—Make a sweetened pie crust, roll thin, and partly bake in sheets; before it is quite done take from the oven, cut in squares of four inches, take up two diagonal corners and pinch together, which makes them basket-shaped; now fill with whipped cream, or white of egg, or both, well sweetened and flavored, and return to oven for few minutes.—Miss Ella Rushton, Atlanta.

Cold Slaw and Dressing.—To 1 quart of chopped cabbage use the following dressing: One teacup of vinegar, 1 teaspoon of mustard, 1 teaspoon of celery seed, 1 teaspoon of salt, 2 tablespoons of sugar, 1 tablespoon of butter; put on the fire and let come to a boil. Beat well 2 eggs, pour on it a cup of sweet milk or cream, add this to the hot dressing, stirring constantly until thick. Pour over cabbage and set away on ice to get cold until ready to serve.—Mrs. D. G. Wylie, Atlanta.

Pop-Up Muffins.—Two cups of milk, 2 cups of flour, 2 eggs and a pinch of salt. Beat eggs separately. Then add flour and milk, a little at a time and beat very hard. Have your tins very hot, and bake at once. The oven must have good bottom heat and yet not too hot, or they will crust over the top before they rise.—Mrs. Kate Cox, Atlanta.

Pineapple Fritters.—Make any nice fritter batter, add 1 grated pineapple.—Mrs. Vannah Dozier, Columbus, Ga.

Cake Without Flour.—One heaping cup of cracker dust, 1 heaping cup of almond dust, 10 eggs, whites and yolks beaten separately. Flavor with vanilla. Cook in layers and spread whipped cream between.—Mrs. Eloise Thomas, Jefferson, Texas.

Nut Cake.—Eight eggs, 2 teacups sugar, ½ pound of English walnuts, 9 tablespoons of cracker dust, 1 teaspoon of spice and cloves; 1 lemon rind grated with the eggs and sugar, very light. Add spices and lemon, cracker dust and nuts; bake in moderate oven.—Mrs. E. Brown, Anderson, S. C.

Velvet Sponge Cake.—Two cups of sugar, 6 eggs, (leave out whites of 3), 1 cup of boiling water, 2½ cups of flour, 1 tablespoon of baking powder in the flour. Beat the yolks of eggs a little. Add the sugar and beat 15 minutes. Add the 3 beaten whites and cup of boiling water just before the flour. Flavor with teaspoon of extract of lemon. Bake in 3 layers, putting between them icing made by adding to the 3 whites, beaten to a stiff froth, 6 dessertspoons of pulverized sugar to each egg. Flavor with lemon. Cooked icing may be used.—Mrs. Charles Lovelace, Columbus, Ga.

Beaten Biscuit.—One pound flour, 3 ounces lard, 1 teaspoon salt, one teacup sweet milk; mix together in very stiff dough, and beat until it blisters and is soft enough to roll out a half inch thick; cut with small cutter, stick each biscuit through with fork, place in moderately hot oven, and bake 25 minutes.—Mrs. S. F. Hamilton, Columbus, Miss.

Salmon Croquettes.—One cup of milk to a can of salmon, 1 spoon of butter rubbed into a dessertspoon of flour. Let the milk come to a boil. Empty the salmon into it, let the whole come to a boil, season and set aside until cold. Mold, dip into raw egg, roll in cracker crumbs and fry in boiling lard.—Mrs. Clifford Anderson, Atlanta.

Tongue Croquettes.—Mix 1 cup of cold tongue chopped fine, 1 cup of cold mashed potatoes; put this mixture in a saucepan, stir over the fire until the potatoes are soft. Add 1 unbeaten egg. Mix carefully, dip in the yellow of 1 egg, roll in cracker dust, make in shapes and fry in boiling lard. —Mrs. B. G. Swanson, LaGrange, Ga.

Cheese Straws.—One pint of grated cheese, ¾ pint of flour, 2 tablespoons of butter, ½ teaspoon of black pepper, a little salt; mix with rich milk or water and bake slowly.—Miss Annie Lou Harralson, Edgewood, Ga.

Nonpariel Cake.—Five eggs, 4 cups of flour, 2 cups of sugar, 1 cup of butter, 1 cup of sweet milk, 2 teaspoons of baking powder (Royal), 1 teaspoon of lemon extract. Beat the eggs separately. Cream the butter and sugar together, add yolks of eggs, then alternately the flour and milk, and lastly the whites of eggs. Mix baking powder in flour.— Mrs. M. Harralson, Edgewood, Ga.

Pop-Ups.—One quart of flour, 2 well-beaten eggs, ¼ teacup of sugar, 1 good-sized yeast cake dissolved in a little milk or water, teaspoon of salt. Mix all well at night, in the morning work in a half cup of butter. Place in a warm stove or near the stove until it rises, then knead it into small biscuits and bake in a quick oven. The eggs must be well beaten, the dough soft with sweet milk.—Mrs. C. A. Ferrell, LaGrange, Ga.

Graham Gems.—One cup sour cream and milk, 2 tablespoons of molasses, 1 egg, ½ teaspoon soda, the same of salt; graham flour to thicken it so that it will drop easily from the spoon. Beat hard and drop into well-heated gem pans, place in a hot oven for 15 or 20 minutes.—Miss Florence Coles, Inman Park.

Flour Muffins.—One quart of flour, 4 eggs, 4 tablespoons of melted butter, 2 cups of sweet milk, 2 heaping teaspoons baking powder, 4 tablespoons of sugar (good without sugar) and salt to taste.—Mrs. Richard Norman, Columbus, Ga.

Punch Sherbet.—Take a quart can of fine peaches; rub through a sieve. Add 1 pint of water, 1 cup of sugar and 1 cup of orange juice. Freeze like a punch and serve in glasses, adding a tablespoon of champagne to each glass when the sherbet is served. The wines served at breakfast are usually sauternes, white Burgundy or claret. It is better form to serve only 1 wine throughout the breakfast than to serve a different wine with each course.—Mrs. Henry L. Wilson, Atlanta.

Orange Souffle.—Whip to a froth 1 quart of sweet rich cream, 4 eggs, well beaten, 1 pint orange juice strained, 14th of a box of gelatine dissolved in a gill of cold water, sugar to your taste. After the gelatine is thoroughly dissolved and the 4 eggs well beaten, pour the gelatine to the eggs, adding the orange juice, then slowly stir in the whipped cream, and sugar to your taste. Then put the whole into freezer, packing ice and salt alternately around the freezer; let stand until firm. Serve in scooped oranges or glass bowl.—Miss Eugenia Rucker, Atlanta.

Boston Brown Bread.—Two cups of corn meal, 1 cup of flour, 1 cup of molasses, 1 cup of sour milk or clabber, a pinch of salt, a level teaspoon of cooking soda dissolved in a little of the sour milk. Sift corn meal and flour together, stirring in molasses, then sour milk, adding salt and soda last. Put in a tight tin bucket or steamer and steam for 4 hours. This requires a hot fire. It can be made one day and dropped in the steamer and heated for use the next day.—Mrs. Robert Paul, McIntosh Co., Ga.

Mush Bread.—Make 1 quart of stiff mush and allow it to cool well, then add 2 or 3 eggs well beaten, ½ tablespoon of lard, ½ tablespoon of soda dissolved in teacup of buttermilk, 2 or 3 tablespoons of meal, salt to taste. When you have plenty of milk use in mush instead of water.—Mrs. James B. Conyers, Cartersville, Ga.

Rusks.—Three cups new milk, 1 cup sugar, 1 cup yeast at night; in the morning 1 cup more of sugar, 1 cup butter; let them rise until light. Cut ½ the recipe into 6 pieces; this will fill 1 dish. When baked, eat with sugar and milk.—Mrs. A. M. Tucker, North Adams, Mass.

Cheese Souffle.—Butter size of an egg, 2 eggs well beaten, ½ cup of milk, 1 pound cheese grated and stirred in last, salt and a dash of cayenne pepper.—Mrs. W. W. Freeman, North Adams, Mass.

Dressing for Slaw.—Three eggs well beaten, 2 level tablespoons of sugar, 1 teaspoon of mustard, 1 teacup of vinegar, a lump of butter the size of a guinea egg. Mix well together. Put on fire, stirring well while cooking to prevent curdling.

When as thick as boiled custard take it off and let cool and then pour over the slaw.—Mrs. Charles T. Hopkins, Atlanta.

Buttermilk Yeast Cakes.—Let 1 pint of buttermilk come to a boil, remove from fire and when tepid, dissolve 1 yeast cake in it and make a thick batter of meal. Let this stand in warm place 5 or 6 hours, or until risen, then add enough meal to make stiff enough to mold into cakes. Dry in the shade, turning frequently. In making bread, use 1 yeast cake (thoroughly dissolved in water with tablespoon of sugar) to 1 quart of flour, heaping tablespoon of lard or butter, a little salt, and water enough to make into a stiff dough. Knead 15 minutes and put to rise in a warm place over night. Make out into rolls or loaves, grease on top and place in well-buttered pans for second rising about 1 hour before baking.—Miss June McKinley, Atlanta.

Caramel Pudding.—Put a handful of loaf sugar to boil in ¼ pint of water until the syrup becomes a deep brown. Warm a small basin, or jelly mold, pour the syrup in it and keep turning the basin in your hand until the inside is completely coated with the syrup, which will by that time have set. Strain the yolks of 8 eggs from the whites, and mix them gradually and effectually with 1 pint of milk. Pour this mixture into the prepared mold, lay a piece of paper on the top; set it in a saucepan of cold water, taking care that the water does not come over the top of the mold; put on the cover and let it boil gently by the side of the fire for 1 hour. Remove the saucepan to a cool place and when the water is quite cold take out the mold and turn the pudding out very carefully. By using a portion of the whites as well as yolks, the risk of breaking the pudding is avoided, but it will not be so delicate.—Mrs. Henry Boylston, Atlanta.

Asper Shade Tea Bread.—One pint of new milk, 1½ pints of flour, 3 eggs beaten separately, 1 cup of yeast (teacup), 1 tablespoon of butter, 1 teaspoon of salt; beat well, let it rise until light; beat again, put into a buttered pan; when well risen, bake.—Mrs. Fannie Whiteside, Atlanta.

Breakfast Cake.—One cup milk, 2 tablespoons sugar, butter the size of an egg, a little salt, 2 eggs, 2 teaspoons baking powder, 3 cups of flour; bake in pans or cups.—Mrs. W. H. Freeman, North Adams, Mass.

White Cake.—One cup butter, 3 cups sugar, 5 cups flour, 5 cups sweet milk, 12 whites of eggs, beaten to a stiff froth; stir butter and sugar together to a cream; sift one teaspoon of baking powder into the flour, and put in the egg whites the last thing; flavor with vanilla extract, bake in a rather moderate oven.—Mrs. N. R. Fowler, Atlanta.

Jelly.—One quart water, 1½ ounces gelatine, 8 ounces of sugar, 1 or 2 lemons, 1 teaspoon of whole mixed spices, 2 whites of eggs and the clean shells; 1 cup of water must be added to allow for evaporation, unless ½ pint of wine is to be used. Put the water in the kettle; add all the other ingredients, the lemon juice without the seeds, and the yellow rind cut very thin, the whites of the eggs beaten a little, and the clean egg shells; set the kettle on the side of the range, and let come to a boil, slowly stirring occasionally; boil 20 minutes, or until the eggs are thoroughly cooked, so that it will mix with the jelly like meal; strain, and if wine is used, put in after straining.—Mrs. E. F. Millitt, Kentucky.

Cough Mixture.—Take buttonwood root and make a strong tea of it; to a pint of the tea and a pint of honey, a piece of saltpetre about the size of your thumb; mix all together and boil down to one pint; also add one tablespoon of paregoric.—Mrs. Marion Wilson, Atlanta.

Green Corn Cake.—One quart grated green corn, 4 eggs, enough flour to make a batter, salt to taste; fry thin on griddle.—Miss Evelyn Orme, Atlanta.

Eastern Shore of Maryland Tea Bread.—Three eggs, 1½ pints warm sweet milk, ¼ cup butter, ½ cup sugar, ½ cup yeast, 1 teaspoon of suet, flour to make a stiff batter; let it stand for 5 hours in a warm place, then stir down; pour into a heated loaf pan and let rise again about half an hour; bake in a moderate oven 50 or 60 minutes; split it open evenly, butter well and place 1 piece on top of the other; send to the table hot.—Miss Bettie McDowell, LaGrange, Ga.

Cheese Bread.—Butter your pan, put in a layer of slices of bread, upon which grate a little cheese; mix together 4 eggs, with 3 cups of sweet milk; pour ½ of it on the first layer of bread and cheese, then put in a second layer of it (and upon the bread put a little butter), and pour upon it the rest of the eggs and milk; bake a short time.—Mrs. Eliza Peeples, Atlanta.

Scotch Cakes.—One cup sugar, 2 cups flour, 1 cup butter, a little spice; rub the butter and sugar together, add flour and spice: roll out and cut with a tumbler; bake on tins.

Champignons or Timbales.—Take 4 eggs, 6 spoons of flour, 1 glass of rum, sugar to suit the taste, stir well; plunge your champignons or timbale iron in the boiling lard;

MISS JUNE McKINLEY,
Member Committee on Agriculture and Horticulture.

when the iron is warm, dip it in the batter, then again into the lard, until the dough is cooked.—Mrs. Marie V. D. Corput, Atlanta.

Creme au Vin Blanc.—Place in a stew pan ½ pint white wine, ¼ pound loaf sugar, flavor with vanilla; allow the mixture to come to a boil; beat the yolks of 8 eggs; add to this 1 tablespoon of arrowroot, mix gradually with the wine; boil this, stirring all the time; pass through a sieve, and allow it to cool.—Miss Mathilde Corput, Atlanta.

Peach Pickle (Sweet).—Seven pounds peaches, peeled, 3 pounds sugar, 1 pint apple vinegar, 2 tablespoons each of allspice, cloves, mace, cinnamon (use the stick cinnamon); tie the different spices up in separate little muslin bags (use whole spices). Put the sugar on the fruit over night; in the morning pour off the juice and heat it scalding hot with the vinegar and spices; pour over the fruit; repeat this for 3 mornings; the fourth morning put the fruit in with the syrup and scald and set away in jars closely covered. After 4 or 5 days examine the fruit and, if there is any signs of fermentation, scald again.—Mrs. W. A. Moore, Atlanta.

Pickled Shrimp.—Take off the heads and fins of the prawn; wash and wipe the prawn dry. Place in jars a layer of prawn and a light layer of salt. Season vinegar strongly with mace and cayenne pepper; scald the vinegar and spices together; when cold, pour over the shrimp or prawn and cover closely.—Miss Bessie Tunno, Charleston, S. C.

Potato Split Biscuit.—Take ½ yeast cake, 1 dessertspoon of brown sugar, ½ cup of milk; dissolve the yeast cake in the milk; take 1 large baked potato, and while hot, mash through a strainer with 1 spoon of butter, 1 egg (beaten very light), a little salt, 1 pint of flour; set to rise; when risen add ½ pint of flour, set to rise again; when risen roll out and make into rolls; rise again and bake.—Mrs. Henry Boylston, Atlanta.

Preventive of Seasickness.—The following remedy, preventive of seasickness, is recommended by Prof. E. Tourgee, of Boston, manager of tourist excursions. It was tried by himself and family, five in all, who had suffered from seasickness on every former voyage across the Atlantic, and in each case it proved entirely successful, and produced no unfavorable results: Dissolve 1 ounce of bromide of sodium in 4 ounces of water; take 1 teaspoon 3 times a day before eating. Begin taking the above 3 days before starting on the sea voyage.—Mrs. Lucy Milner Lumpkin, Atlanta.

Fruit Cake.—Two pounds raisins, seeded and cut in 2 pieces; 2 pounds currants, washed clean in a sieve and dried in the sun; 1 pound citrons, 1 pound flour, 1 pound sugar, ¾ of a pound of butter, 10 eggs, one tumbler of wine or brandy. I use also ½ tumbler of syrup from sweet pickles, 2 tablespoons of cinnamon, 1 of cloves, 1 nutmeg. After the raisins have been seeded and cut, pour brandy or wine on them, and let stand over night. Do this with all the fruit. After weighing the flour, take some of it and rub on the fruit; after mixing your cake, add your fruit; if the batter is too thin the fruit will sink to the bottom of the pan; bake slowly for 3 hours; if very thick, will take 4 hours.—Mrs. John Morse, Atlanta.

Coffee Cake.—Scald ½ of a cup of milk, add to it ½ of a cup of cold water, a very small piece of butter, ½ teaspoon of salt, and the same of sugar; when lukewarm, add ¼ cup of yeast, and enough flour to make a stiff batter; beat until smooth; let stand over night, or until light; then add enough flour to make a soft dough; knead for 10 minutes, until very smooth and velvety, being very careful not to add too much flour, as it must be very soft; let rise until it has doubled its bulk; beat 3 tablespoons of butter to a cream, add 4 heaping tablespoons of sugar and beat again, adding 1 egg beaten light, without separating; work this into the dough very thoroughly, then set aside to raise; when light, pour into a well-greased baking pans and bake 25 minutes in a moderately quick oven. While the cake is baking, prepare an icing with the whites of 2 eggs, and 2 tablespoons of powdered sugar; beat the whites only until they begin to be light; add the sugar by degrees, then beat until smooth and glossy. When the cake is done, spread with the icing, and put in the oven to dry for 2 minutes.—Mrs. Henry L. Wilson, Atlanta.

Charlotte Russe.—One quart of cream, whites of 3 eggs, 9 tablespoons of sugar; flavor with sherry wine, ½ cup of gelatine, pour upon it boiling water until the cup is full. When the gelatine is well dissolved and cooled, mix with cream, eggs, etc., and then churn.—Miss Kate Harralson, Edgewood, Ga.

Spiced Apples.—Eight pounds apples, peeled and cored, 4 pounds sugar, 1 quart vinegar, 1 ounce stick cinnamon, ½ ounce whole cloves; boil vinegar, sugar and spice together;

while boiling, add apples, a half at a time; boil until tender, twenty minutes will suffice; remove and add others, until all have been in jar; boil syrup until thick as you like, and pour over; should there be too little to cover the fruit, sweeten and scald enough vinegar to thoroughly cover the apples; cover jar with a wax cloth.—Mrs. A. D. Adair, Atlanta.

Boiled Plum Pudding.—Two tumblers of fine bread crumbs, 1 tumbler of sifted flour, ½ pound raisins, seeded and cut in half, the same of currants, picked and dried; a large piece of citron, cut into strips; chop ½ pound of dried beef suet, soak several hours in a tumbler of brandy or wine; 1 tablespoon of mace and cinnamon, mixed; add to the butter 1 beaten nutmeg, 2 grated lemons, removing the seed; 10 eggs, beaten well, with a tumbler of sugar; pour upon the bread 2 tumblers of rich milk, very hot; tie well, and follow the directions for boiling; serve with a rich sauce.—Mrs. McD. Dunwoody.

A New Chicken Salad.—One quart of chicken cut into dice, 2 large cucumbers, 1 can of French peas; chop the cucumbers and let drain; turn the peas into a colander, let cold water run over them for a moment, and then dry in a cloth; just before serving, mix all together with a very thick salad dressing, either a boiled dressing or a mayonnaise. This salad is most delicious, far better than the salad made with chicken and celery.—Mrs. C. L. Russell, Cleveland, Ohio.

Canelon of Beef.—Two pounds of the round of the beef, chopped very fine, also 3 sprigs of parsley chopped fine; 1 heaping teaspoon of salt, 1 tablespoon of butter, ½ teaspoon of black pepper, 1 raw egg, and ⅓ teaspoon of onion juice; add these ingredients to the minced beef and parsley and mix thoroughly. Shape into a roll about 3 inches in diameter. Roll in a buttered paper, place in a baking pan and pour over it boiling water (which will melt the butter), basting meat quite often to keep paper from burning. When cooked done enough, place on a hot dish, unroll from the paper, and serve with tomato sauce made as follows: Stew a pint of tomatoes, half a slice of onion and 4 cloves together 10 minutes. Put on to cook 1 heaping tablespoon of butter in a small frying pan; when it is brown add 1 tablespoon of flour, stir constantly for 2 or 3 minutes, then add a teaspoon of salt, ½ teaspoon of white pepper or few grains of cayenne to the tomatoes. Rub all through a wire strainer to keep back seeds. Pour this around the beef pone and garnish with parsley.—Mrs. John W. Hurt, Atlanta.

Fanchonettes.—Bake nice pastry in scallop shells or patty pans; place an almond macaroon in center of each; cover with red fruit jelly, then with a thin layer of meringue. Fill a paper funnel with stiff meringue, drop a circle of cones an inch in height and diameter around it, and one in the center; set in the oven until colored very slightly. When cold, surmount each cone with a tiny fragment of red jelly or some pretty and delicate confection. An elegant dessert.—Mrs. S. A. Sykes, Aberdeen, Miss.

Citron Pudding.—Line your pie plates with thin paste; cut the citron in thin slices and cover bottom of plates; mix together the yolks of 8 eggs and whites of 2 beaten separately, a half pound of sugar, and a half pound of melted butter; beat this mixture well, and pour it over citron; bake in a moderate oven; beat the 6 whites and 5 tablespoons of sugar until smooth; pour over top of pudding after it is baked; put in stove and brown lightly.—Mrs. J. D. Shell, Aberdeen, Miss.

Pumpkin Chips.—From a highly colored pumpkin cut slices about 3 inches long and 1 inch broad, and about the thickness of a dollar; for 1 pound of chips, 1 pound of sugar; pare the rinds of 5 lemons and add the juice, allowing 1 gill of juice to 1 pound of chips. Put the pumpkin into a bread pan and cover with the sugar. Pour the lemon juice over it and let stand all night. Boil all together till the pumpkin is clear; half an hour is sufficient. When half boiled, take out the pumpkin, let it cool, return it and boil till clear.— Mrs. Henry Boylston, Atlanta.

Florida Orange Marmalade.—Six perfect oranges with bright skin, 2 lemons, 4 pounds of sugar. With a sharp knife shred the oranges and lemons as fine as possible, removing the seed with the cutting. Put the shredded fruit in an earthen or porcelain vessel and add a half gallon of water. Cover and let stand 48 hours. Pour the whole into a preserving kettle, add the 4 pounds of sugar. Let it boil until the fruit becomes transparent and a little jellied. The more quickly it is cooked, the more brilliant the color.— Emma Moffett Tyng.

Swedish Prune Pudding.—Take the pits of ½ pound of French prunes. Steam the prunes until tender and chop them fine. Take the meats out of pits and chop fine. Mix together the prunes, chopped meats and 6 tablespoons of powdered sugar, and the beaten whites of 10 eggs. Bake immediately, 15 minutes, and serve with whipped cream. Do not grease the tin, but pour cold water in it before putting in the pudding.—Mrs. Archibald Davis, Atlanta.

Fruit Conserve.—Five pounds currants, 3 pounds sugar, 2 oranges, 1 pound raisins, seeded; use grated rind, juice and pulp of the oranges, freed from the white skin and the seeds; cook the whole about 20 minutes; if the seeds of the currants are objectionable, strain them, using only the juice, and add cherries, equal in bulk to the discarded currant seeds.—Mrs. W. D. Shuart, Rochester, N. Y.

Ginger Pears.—Eight pounds of pears, weighed after they are pared, and cut into dice; 6 pounds granulated sugar, 4 large lemons, ½ pound green ginger root; peel lemons, and chop the pulp and yellow rind, discarding the white inner skin; parboil the ginger root to soften, and cut into bits; cook all together, adding one quart of water, for 3 hours, or until the consistency of jelly when cold.—Mrs. W. D. Shuart, Rochester, N. Y.

Onion and Cucumber Pickle.—Slice 1 peck cucumbers, and ½ peck onions; let stand over night in salt; in the morning, wash off the salt, and in a stone jar put a layer of onions, then one of cucumbers, sprinkling over each layer whole pepper, mustard seed, and a little powdered cinnamon; continue this until the jar is almost full, then to ½ gallon vinegar add 1 pint port wine, and ½ pint olive oil, and pour the whole over the pickle; every morning, for two weeks, stir well.—Miss Stella Shuart, Rochester, N. Y.

Dutch Lettuce (For the Chafing Dish.)—Two heads of lettuce, shredded; ¼ pound raw ham, diced; 1 egg, raw; dash of pepper, either cayenne or paprika; 2 tablespoons vinegar, 2 tablespoons sour cream; put ham in blazer over the flame, and cook until brown, and the fat well dried out; then add the vinegar, pepper, broken egg, and sour cream, stirring constantly until it thickens; add the shredded lettuce, and serve hot.—Miss Stella Shuart, Rochester, N. Y.

Apple Salad.—Two tart apples, 1 cup celery, juice of one lemon; pare apples and cut into dice, add celery and lemon juice; pour over this a French dressing made from 3 tablespoons of oil, one tablespoon of vinegar, ¼ teaspoon salt, ⅛ teaspoon pepper; serve on lettuce leaves, with chopped parsley and mayonnaise dressing, 1 teaspoon of the latter being added to each little nest of the salad.—Miss Gertrude Shuart, Rochester, N. Y.

Beet Salad.—One cup boiled beets, diced; 1 cup boiled potatoes, diced; 1 cup celery, diced; ½ teaspoon celery salt, ½ teaspoon curry powder; pour over this a dressing, made as follows: One tablespoon sugar, ½ teaspoon salt, 1 cup vinegar, 3 eggs; beat all together, boil until it begins to thicken like custard, then add one cup sour milk, stirring constantly; let boil five minutes more, and when cold, pour over the vegetables.—Miss Stella Shuart, Rochester, N. Y.

Ginger Wafers.—One-half cup butter washed and creamed, ½ cup sweet milk, 1 cup fine brown sugar (sifted), 2 cups flour sifted twice, 1 heaping tablespoon ground ginger. Rub the bottom of stove pans with cold butter and spread the mixture as thin as paper; bake in moderate oven. When browned, cut into squares with sharp knife; remove immediately from pan. (Very crisp and nice.)—Mrs. F. B. Mapp, Milledgeville, Ga.

Washington Pie.—One tablespoon butter, ½ cup sugar, 1 cup flour, 1 teaspoon baking powder, ½ cup sweet milk, 1 egg. Cream butter and sugar, beat in yolk, add flour and milk, lastly white of egg, bake in 2 layers, spread between jelly or jam, serve hot with egg sauce.

Egg Sauce.—One-half cup sugar, ½ cup water. Cook without stirring until it ropes, turn slowly into the beaten white of 1 egg, juice of ½ lemon, tablespoon of jelly; beat well.—Mrs. F. B. Mapp, Milledgeville, Ga.

Chicken Salad.—The white meat of a cold boiled or roasted chicken, ¾ of the same bulk of chopped celery (or of crisp, white cabbage if the celery is not to be had), 2 hard-boiled eggs (only using yolks), 1 raw egg well beaten in Dover egg-beater, 1 teaspoon of salt, 1 teaspoon of mustard (to taste), pepper, 3 teaspoons of salad oil, 2 teaspoons white sugar, ½ teacup of vinegar or what is still better, lemon juice. Directions: Rub the yolks to fine powder (it helps to put a little butter to it). Add the salt, pepper and sugar; then the oil, grinding hard, putting in a few drops at a time. Add the mustard next and let all stand while you whip the raw egg to a froth. Beat this into the dressing and pour in the vinegar (or lemon juice) spoonful by spoonful, whipping the dressing well while you do it. Sprinkle a little dry salt over the meat and celery. Pour the dressing over it. Mix it well.—Mrs. Sarah Cooper Sanders, Washington, Ga.

Remedy for Croup.—One pint of olive oil, 1 ounce of gum camphor (pulverized), 2 ounces of white wax. Pour the olive oil into a covered vessel, place it over the fire, add the gum camphor and let slowly boil until the camphor is all dissolved, then add the wax, stirring thoroughly, until melted. Pour the contents of the vessel into glass jars and screw the tops firmly down. Keep in a dark place. This salve is to be used as a plaster over the throat and chest. In my own experience I have found it to be a most excellent remedy for croup. It is also very good for asthma.—Mrs. D. N. Speer, Atlanta.

Gumbo Soup.—Cut a spring chicken and a small slice of ham into small pieces; into a pot put a heaping tablespoon of lard; when quite hot, put in the ham and chicken, and fry brown; add to this 2 large tomatoes, 1 onion, 1 tablespoon of flour; let brown a little; add 3 dozen okra cut into small pieces. Cover with sufficient water to make required quantity of soup; let simmer over slow fire, salt to taste; serve with boiled rice; cook 2 or 3 hours, and if too thick, ½ an hour before serving, thin with boiling water.—Miss Daisy Hodgson, New Orleans.

Green Tomato Sweet Pickles.—Slice the tomatoes and onions and put into a jar with thick layers of salt; let remain over night. The next morning wash thoroughly in cold water and squeeze dry; cover with vinegar, and to every gallon add the following: ½ pound of sugar, 1 ounce of celery seed, ¼ pound of mustard, 1 ounce of allspice, 1 ounce black pepper, 2 nutmegs; boil the whole gently until clear and tender; put some turmeric in muslin bag to color pickle.— Mrs. Ira E. Fort, Atlanta.

Walnut Salad.—Crack 25 English walnuts and pick out the kernels as whole as possible; cover with the juice of lemon and let stand for 2 hours; do not drain, but pick them out of the lemon juice and serve on watercress with French dressing. The English serve the green walnuts as a salad, and the nuts are often soaked in wine in preference to lemon juice.—Mrs. Wm. Hoyle, Atlanta.

French Dressing for Salads.—Two tablespoons of olive oil, 4 of vinegar in a soup plate where a teaspoon of scraped raw onion has been placed, then olive oil, vinegar and red pepper pulverized; add black pepper and a little salt; serve the leaves of bleached lettuce on plates at the seat of each person at the table, placing at least a whole, hard-boiled egg cut in half in the middle of each plate for a garnishing with the lettuce leaves turned to the middle; then serve the dressing over the lettuce; it is better than a mayonnaise.—Mrs. E. P. Pullen, Atlanta.

Jam Cake.—Two cups of flour, ¾ cup of butter, 1 cup of sugar, 8 eggs, 3 tablespoons of sour cream, 1 teaspoon of soda, 1 teaspoon spice, 1 teaspoon nutmeg, 1 teaspoon cinnamon, 2 cups of jam last. This is equal to a black fruit cake.—Mrs. Robert W. Walker, Marysville, Tenn.

Gentlemen's Favorite Cake.—Seven eggs, whites and yolks beaten separately; 2 cups sugar, ½ cup of butter worked to a cream, 1 tablespoon of water, 2 teaspoons of baking powder, 2 cups flour, ½ teaspoon of salt; bake in jelly cake pan. Jelly for the same: One egg, 1 cup of sugar, 3 apples, peeled and grated, juice of one lemon; stir until it thickens and cool before using.—Mrs. Dr. R. L. Sykes, Columbus, Miss.

Coffee Jelly.—One-half box Knox's gelatine, soak in 1 cup cold water for 1 hour, then add 1 cup boiling water, 1 cup sugar and 2 cups cold coffee.—Miss Louise Galuph, North Adams, Mass.

Snow Cheese.—One and one-half ounce sweet almonds, 1 tablespoon of ratifia, 2 tablespoons of rose water, 1 quart of cream, juice of 3 lemons, 3 ounces of sugar; blanch the almonds and pound, add the ratifia and rose water, stir it into the quart of cream, add the strained juice of the lemons and sugar; whisk the mixture until it begins to thicken; pour nuts in the mold and set to cool. It will be ready in 12 hours.—Mrs. F. F. Lyden, Baltimore, Md.

Egg Timbales.—For 6 persons use ½ dozen eggs, 3 gills of milk, 1 teaspoon of salt, ⅛ of a teaspoon of pepper, 1 teaspoon of chopped parsley and ¼ of a teaspoon of onion juice; break the eggs into a bowl and beat them well with a fork, then add the seasoning and beat for a minute longer. Now add the milk and stir well. Butter 8 timbale molds of medium-size and pour the mixture into them. Put the molds in a deep pan and pour in enough hot water to come almost to the top of the molds. Place in a moderate oven and cook until firm in the center; about 20 minutes; then turn out on a warm dish and pour a cream or tomato sauce around them. This is a nice dish for breakfast, luncheon or tea.—Mrs. J. D. Collins, Atlanta.

Queen of Puddings.—Eight eggs, pint of milk, pound of sugar, 4 spoons of flour or corn starch and a pinch of salt, heaping spoon of butter, flavor with vanilla; put the milk and nearly all the sugar and butter on to boil; mix flour with a little cold water until a smooth paste, then beat into it the yolks of the eggs; add the salt; while the milk is boiling have the whites beaten stiff, adding only enough sugar to sweeten delicately, more will cause meringue to fall; beat the yolks of eggs and flour into the boiling milk and sugar; as soon as it thickens pour into pudding bowl and place the whites on top; bake slowly till meringue is a light brown.—Miss Martha Harris, High Shoals, Ga.

Orange Pudding.—Grate rind and squeeze the juice of 2 oranges or lemons; stir together with ½ pound of butter, ½ pound of sugar and a wineglass of mixed wine and brandy; beat 6 eggs very light and gradually add them; bake ½ hour; when cool grate sugar over it.—Mrs. Dora Adams Hopkins, Atlanta.

Old-Fashioned Mince Meat.—Four pounds of tender beef, 1½ pounds suet, 8 pounds chopped apples, 3 pounds currants, washed, dried and picked, 3 pounds seeded raisins, 6 pounds sugar (brown will do), 2 pounds citron (chopped), 2 pounds large oranges (grated rind, juice and pulp), 4 large lemons (ditto), 1 ounce of cinnamon, ¼ ounce of cloves (ground), ¼ ounce of mace, ¼ ounce of allspice, 4 nutmegs (grated), 1 quart Madeira wine, 1 pint brandy, 1 cup of strawberry or raspberry jam, 1 cup of quince preserves, 2 cups of molasses, 2 cups of vinegar, salt to taste; use the water that the meat was boiled in and cook as long as you see fit.—Mrs. L. P. Leary, Atlanta.

Beef Tea (For Invalids).—One-half pound tender beef (no fat), cut in bits; put in glass bottles, with top well screwed on (can add a little water), place in kettle of boiling water

20 minutes, take out, shake well; this quantity makes 1 cup of rich tea.—Mrs. George B. Heard, LaGrange, Ga.

French Biscuits.—Make a light dough with sweet milk and baking powder; roll thin and dot with small pieces of fresh, sweet butter, sprinkle sugar over all and roll; cut in pieces an inch thick and place in biscuit pan; let rise in a warm place about 5 minutes and bake in quick oven; powdered cinnamon, nutmeg or any other spices may be sprinkled in with the sugar, according to taste.—Miss Mattie Elkin, Lancaster, Ky.

Gumbo for 3 O'clock Dinner (Six Plates).—1 chicken fried and bones mashed, 3 slices ham fried and minced, 1 pint dried okra, 3 tomatoes, egg size, 1 onion, 1 handful parsley, 1 large tablespoon lard, 1 green pepper, 1 kettle of boiling water, 1 tablespoon flour, salt and pepper to taste; have the pot in which you wish to make your gumbo on the stove hot at 10 o'clock A. M., and put in the lard; when it is boiling, stir in the flour immediately, and quickly stir in the onions, parsley, tomatoes, green pepper, all having been previously cut up together; then drop in the okra, stirring all the time, pour in boiling water, and season with salt and pepper to your taste; stew all well, cover it and let it boil pretty hard for half an hour (but not over a blaze), then slower and slower; at 12 o'clock, put in the chicken and ham; occasionally stir the gumbo until ready to serve, with rice.—Mrs. Anna B. Nickles, Laredo, Texas.

Sponge Cake Roll.—Four eggs, beaten separately, 1 teacup sugar, 1 teacup flour, 1 teaspoon cream tartar mixed in the flour, ½ teaspoon soda in a little water; bake quickly in a biscuit pan, turn out on a damp towel, put jelly between, and serve while warm.—Mrs. G. W. D. Cook, Atlanta.

Puff Pudding.—Ten tablespoons flour, 3 cups milk, 4 eggs, 1 teaspoon melted butter; bake 20 minutes in square tins. Sauce for Pudding: One-half cup butter, 1 cup sugar, mix well together, add 1 cup boiling milk, flavor with wine or vanilla.—Mrs. C. A. Nichols, Springfield, Mass.

Croutons.—Slice some stale bread, remove the crust, cut in small dice, heat some butter in a pan on the fire; when it is boiling, drop in the bread; shake frequently till light golden brown; the butter should nearly cover the bread; when done, in about 1 minute, remove with a skimmer to brown paper in the open mouth of the oven; when dry, serve on a cut paper at the same time with tomato soup, or any other puree. —Mrs. E. A. Angier, Atlanta.

Corn Muffins.—One pint sifted meal and 3 gills milk, 1 pint sour milk, or 1 gill sour cream, 2 tablespoons boiling hot lard, 2 eggs, 1 teaspoon soda, ½ cup sugar; add the eggs, beaten separately, to meal and milk; pour on lard, boiling hot.—Miss Sawyer, Sapelo Island, McIntosh Co., Ga.

Lemon Sauce.—The whites of 2 eggs, beaten, with 1 cup of white sugar. Pour on it 1 cup of boiling milk. Just before serving add the juice of a lemon.—Mrs. W. C. Glenn, Atlanta.

White Cake.—The whites of 4 eggs, 2 cups of flour, 1 cup sugar, ½ cup butter, ½ cup of milk, 1 teaspoon of yeast powder.—Mrs. Mary Cook, Atlanta.

Turtle Soup.—Three teaspoons of cinnamon (ground), 3 teaspoons of mace, 1 teaspoon of brown sugar, ⅛ teaspoon of spice, 1 heaping teaspoon of butter, ½ tumbler of pepper vinegar, ½ tumbler of sherry or Madeira wine, salt, 1 dozen eggs boiled hard and cut up, a little brown flour to thicken it, 6 onions (medium size) cut up fine and boiled with the turtle. Take the turtle out of the soup, pick out the bones, and put the turtle, cut up fine, back in soup. Canned turtle will do, using 2 cans for above proportions and putting in a little piece of fat bacon about 3 inches square. The brand of canned turtle is best with green turtle on box.—Mrs. E. P. Howell, West End.

Chocolate Caramel Cake.—One cup butter, 2 cups sugar, 3 cups flour, 4 eggs, 1 cup milk, 2 scant spoons of yeast powder; bake in 3 layers. Let the middle layer be heavily spiced, with 2 tablespoons brandy added. Filling: Two cups sugar, ½ cup butter, ½ cup milk, ½ cup water, spoonful vanilla, section of chocolate; boil until quite thick, stiring all the time, and beat until nearly cold.—Mrs. David W. Appler, Atlanta.

Dainty Dinner or Tea Rolls.—Roll out pie crust dough ¼ inch thick, cut in pieces 3 inches wide, 6 inches long; spread first with butter, then add a layer of apple jelly; roll and bake; nice, hot or cold.—Mrs. Julia M. Watson, Atlanta.

Vermicelli Toast.—One cup of milk, ½ cup of flour, ½ teaspoon of salt, 3 full teaspoons of butter; boil milk, mix in flour and butter; boil 3 eggs hard, chop whites, put whites into this sauce and pour over toasted bread, grating the yellows of eggs over top of this. A little parsley added is good. —Miss Mattie Smith, Griffin, Ga.

INDEX.

	PAGES.
Soups	5-8
Oysters and Fish	9-13
Meats	13-24
Pickles	25-28
Vegetables	28-33
Salads	33-39
Bread	39-46
Cakes	47-63
Puddings and Custards	63-78
Gelatines	78-85
Chafing Dish Recipes	85-90
Frozen Desserts	90-100
Confectionery	100-104
Beverages	104-111
Menus	112-113
P. S.	114-148

Odorless Refrigerator

TRADE MARK

PATENTED JULY, 1896

Onions, Bananas, all kinds of Fruits, Meats, Fish, Cheese and everything that has an Odor, can be put together with Milk and Butter and

One Dish Won't Taste of Another
A GREAT ICE SAVER
NEEDS NO WASHING OUT

MRS. SARAH TYSON RORER says:

"I am using a refrigerator of this make in my school-room, keeping it, or rather crowding it, with all kinds of materials. I find that the ventilation is so perfect that even the milk and butter are not contaminated by foods with odors. Of course, I have been using this refrigerator for a year without scrubbing or scalding it."

If your dealer has not got it, write to

The Keyser Manufacturing Co.
SEND FOR CATALOGUE   CHATTANOOGA, TENN.

Can recommend above refrigerator. Am now using it and find it all that is claimed.—MRS. HENRY L. WILSON.

www.ingramcontent.com/pod-product-compliance
Lightning Source LLC
Chambersburg PA
CBHW020800160426
43192CB00006B/391